Millionaire Habits

Master the secret habits of Millionaires for wealth and prosperity

by

Edgar Allan

Table Of Contents

Part 1
Understanding Habits — 5

Your Guide To Automatic Success - Your Habits Define You — 7

Are You Sabotaging Your Own Success? Habits That Hinder Success — 9

Understand Your Connection With Your Brain — 11

Do You Know How Habits Are Formed ? — 13

Brace Your Subconscious For Success — 15

Learn How to Save Money Now in Order to Invest in a More Financially Secure Future! — 22

Did You Get High On Self-Enhancement? You Need To Constantly Evolve! — 24

Can You Feel Better By Just Doing Nothing? Practice Motivation! — 26

This Will Make Your Success Inevitable – Connect With Successful People — 27

The Truth About Successful Persons — 31

Rich Habits vs. Poor Habits — 32

Part 2 — 34

Millionaire Habits – Is It A Mindset? — 34

Success Is The Only Path That Matters — 35

You Should Know This — 37

What Do You Think About Wealth ? — 40

Are You Ready To Create More Wealth? — 40

The Paths Towards Growth — 42

The Secret To Your Success Is Hidden In Your Life Story — 44

Part 3 — 47

Your Chance To Be Your Own Hero — 47

The Success Strategy No One Talks About — 48

Your Life's Work Is Hidden Here — 49

Don't Wait To Grow Your Earnings – Automate The Process — 51

The Key To The Greatest Success Stories Ever — 52

Self-Sabotaging Beliefs? Kill tThem And Choose YOU! — 52

Do You Know Your Life Code? — 54

How To Change Your Entire Life - Create Meaningful Life Experiences — 55

The Real Reason You're not Making More — 56

Uncommon Strategies For Sustainable Success — 57

The Fastest Way To Heal You - Live A Full And Satisfying Life — 58

Feel Inspired And Creative — 60

This Will Double, Triple And Quadruple Your Growth — 62

Part 4 — 64

Did You Get On The Ladder To Success — 64

Find Your Team – It's Imperative — 67

Find Yourself A Mentor — 68

A Few Critical, Often Overlooked, Steps To Lasting Success — 69

Millionaire Success Practice - How To Overcome Any Obstacle — 70

Create Your To Do List – Everything Else Goes On Not To Do List — 72

Make A Living Doing What You Love – And Inspire Others — 73

Fall Down 7. Get Up 8 — 74

The What If Game — 76

Make A Living Doing What You Love   76

30 Ways That Makes The Rich Different   78

Learnt The Success Habits? Apply Them Next – That's The Only Way Forward   79

Become Part Of A Mastermind Group   80

Rich Habits – Busting The Myths   81

And Some Success Stories   82

References   86

Copyright 2019 by Edgar Allan - All rights reserved.

The content of this book is meant to serve as a summary and analysis of the original book. This book is not designed to be used as a substitute to the original book. However, it is designed to enrich the reading experience by providing the key ideas and concepts in an easy-to-remember structure. Also, the book is not authorized, approved, endorsed or licensed by the author of the original book.

No part of this book may be copied, changed or transmitted in any shape or making use of any strategies, such as photocopying, recording, or different electronic or mechanical systems, without the previous made approval out of the distributor, beside through distinctive feature of short references embodied in critical overviews and positive other non-commercial usages permitted via copyright regulation.

The information given is communicated to be truthful and unsurprising, in that any risk, in addition as loss of regard or something one of a kind, by using any use or abuse of any methodologies, methodology, or path contained interior is the single and comprehensible responsibility of the recipient peruser. In no way, shape or form will any actual dedication or blame be held towards the distributor for any reparations, hurts, or financial mishap due to the information in this way, either direct or round aboutly.

The statistics in this is supplied for instructional functions entirely, and is general as so. The presentation of the statistics is without contract or any form of accreditation confirmation.

The trademarks used in this book are without the consent or permission from the trademark owner (or the author of the original book). All the trademarks used within this book are for educational purposes only and are not affiliated with this document.

Part 1
Understanding Habits

A lot of research has been done to help us understand what habits are, how they are formed, and how you can use them to your advantage. This book will enhance your understanding of some everyday habits, and how your habits can bring you success with lasting breakthroughs in your life. Not only will you find the hidden secrets of millionaire habits, but also undergo a journey of change because the power you are searching for lies within you.

Irrespective of your beliefs, you are a powerhouse who can change your life the way you want. To go from mediocrity to wealth, you need three basic things.

1. Daily growth
2. Motivational focus
3. Persistence

Referring to these three as the basic success traits, this book will guide you towards acquisition of these traits. By definition, habits are routines that are persistent. Habits are exhibited in the recurring occurrence of events in your daily life. While there are good and bad habits that determine your success, they tend to have a cumulative effect. Acting as an investment that adds to your long term vision, it is imperative to steer your habit seesaw in the right direction. You can't imagine how empowering it is to gain control over your habits. A research on happiness found that the feeling of being in control of your life is a fundamental factor in the creation of happiness (). Not only do they pave the way for your success, your habits determine the quality of life you live. Brace yourselves, for your life is about to change for the better.

What you're about to discover in this book will change your life forever and put you on the road to success. If you pay close attention, you will disclose the patterns that have been sabotaging your success. Beware – those are the habits that have kept you from achieving success.

According to modern brain science, there is _one_ force that shapes your career and financial success more than anything else. Hint: It's not how many hours you work every week. It's not how self-motivated you are. And it's not even the books you read or the seminars you've attended.

It's your direction and we believe with the right direction, you can do anything.

Truth be told, here we are talking beyond the 'think and act' philosophy, because while thoughts and actions are important, the secret that actually makes it work are the rightly steered actions. That's when you start manifesting your truest potential. In this book, you will:

- End self-sabotage, procrastination, and many other negative habits
- Get out of overwhelm, burnout, and become unstuck forever
- Turn every relationship conflict into greater strength and empowerment
- Reclaim all the energy you've been wasting on this inner battle
- Unlock your natural wealth and abundance that the shadows are blocking
- Gain the clarity and confidence of purpose being obscured by the shadows
- Activate the self-worth to ask for what you need, have strong boundaries, and go for what you really want without shame, blame, or apology!
- Wake up and walk through your day loving ALL OF YOU (can you imagine the power of that? It's a game-changer!)

And so much more!

Your Guide To Automatic Success - Your Habits Define You

What is life? The answer to this question will lead you to explore thousands of possibilities you might come across in your daily existence. Put simply, life is the single most precious gift that is often cared the least for by most of us. Overseeing the numerous blessings one has been bestowed with, life goes on like this and it is often the death bed when one realizes the true worth of what has gone by. Our routine habits are mundane and ordinary. This fact makes it pretty evident that the need to realize that 'missing factor' is crucial have you been wishing to live well. Living well is undoubtedly the most desired of all things – whether you admit it or not! And this is only possible if you change your habits.

Life often gives you so much that it gets difficult to take account of everything and pay attention to it. Also very often, some surprising events take place which leave you astonished. Thus, life pertains to be a mixture of the good and bad surprises – or a series of habits. However, majority of the time what needs the most consideration is the recurrence of unwanted events. Not when they happen, but after they have happened. Do they reflect patterns from your routine? Are they the unwanted chunks piled up?

They usually leave you with their negative embankments and before you realize it, it's too late. This means that unexpected things are responded to unexpectedly. These submissive thoughts form your actions are evocative of your whole character. Therefore, you emerge as one of the naïve personalities around who can only see the negative. Before this situation turns into something worse, you need to address it immediately in order to boost yourself with the much needed confidence and make this world a better place.

The process starts with self-actualization. Once you understand your personality and accept that you are having a hard time coming up with positive habits, only then we can proceed further. Having understood this, as soon as you accept this fact about your very own self can you further take any measures to change your life – rather reinvent it!

Acknowledge that you are now amongst those negative people out there you had never imagined to become; whom you were against. This will make things much easier and enable you to look in the correct direction. Acceptance is the first initiative you take towards reinventing your life. Once accepted, you are now headed towards the right path and this path will enable you to accomplish what you really need to be – a reinvented person with habits that are wired for success.

This book will introduce you to habits in a new way, helping you feel better, giving you a new perspective of thinking and seeing things, showing you techniques to better interact with yourself and with others, and last but not the least, put you on the road to success. Let's now consider the whole process in detail so once you have understood it, you can get a hold of your life, drive in the positive direction and get going. This will precisely mark the beginning of the fact that you are on your way to reinvent your life!

Now that you have left all the negativity behind, have jumped out of your discouraging thoughts, are suggesting the good to yourself and are empowered with a boost of positive energy, you are all ready to set your objectives and self-goals.

As you are empowered, you have the desired ability of controlling your life and its purpose. Your aptitude defines your objectives and your self-esteem is developed to a level that it settles for no less than what you actually deserve. You now know what you are capable of doing and what you deserve. Thus, you become clear regarding your objectives and tend to stay away from all those possibilities that can bring you down. This is because you are focused and want to attain your goals at any cost.

Are You Sabotaging Your Own Success? Habits That Hinder Success

You might not be surprised to know that negativity is a psychological phenomenon that seeds up in the brain because of unpleasant event or events. The happenings of events that are not in accordance with your desires often make you resentful. This makes you perceive things in a negative manner. It is important to note that there are always two sides to perceiving anything. One face of it is what you want to see, the other is the real thing. Your perception does not allow you to let go of things and the negative feelings in your mind grow. Things get worse when this negativity stems into the thinking process and hence, you tend to experience a negative outburst. Your actions, gestures, preferences, dealings and your overall life get affected.

To sum up the consequences, negativity is a self-contagious thing, which if left unchecked, can start invading your thinking process and ultimately habits. It has a deeply adverse influence on your life and you soon realize your potential to be eaten up. The creativity in you dies and you start losing all the confidence you once had. Your personality begins to shatter and you are unable to come up with ideas. Thus, an ever increasing pessimistic stance is invoked and you can barely see any good in your surroundings.

The health also gets affected and you get to experience disturbed metabolic activity which ceases the digestive power, hence body is provided with little energy. Moreover, anxiety jumps in which makes you feel restless all the time. Tachycardia, sore muscles and bone loss also result due to the negative stance. All of these factors combined might cause a feeling of disturbance, discomfort and even paranoia, and before you know it, it is often too late.

The impact of these negative vibes on your life makes you weak from within, and thus you start to feel lethargic and weak. This drains the devotion in you and you fail to meet your desired objectives. You get susceptible to diseases.

Negativity sprouts from your behavior which leads to a feeling of aggression. You start to make pessimistic statements which are felt by those around you. This pessimistic stance inculcates the negativity in you and you start to think of the bad aspects of anything first. Distrustfulness enters into your life and you display vivid characteristics of pessimism. The cycle continues and your social life gets severely affected. Your interaction with people start to get weak and thus, your personality starts to lose all the charisma. What was an otherwise successful life starts to decline that directly affects your social standing. You start entailing a closed mindset which is not taking you anywhere.

As a consequence, you come up with a mindset which has shut the doors of suggestions upon itself. You are not willing to hear anything that is not according to your mood and that is why when something is suggested to you, you tend to dismiss it outright, and therefore, you might be seem proud. All of this when combined with the previous list of things gives you an even negative reputation which is certainly something you don't want!

If you desperately want to improve your condition and shed this reputation, then the first thing you need to do is to open up, and this process starts with thinking.

Understand Your Connection With Your Brain

As already described, a closed mind clogs your thinking process and you fail to remain open to any good upcoming possibilities. In order to negate the negativity you have encountered up till now is to start thinking in a positive manner. Positive thinking is not just a simple stream of thoughts – it is a consistent and conscious effort towards seeing everything from a whole new perspective. While you tend to change things with the mind first, your actions will speak loudly of the change you have accepted and thereby, you have already started your journey towards reinvention.

The first and foremost rule of changing your thinking process is to start doing well to yourself. YOU are more important than anything, and unless you realize this fact, you can't move ahead. Once you understand that everything you have to do starts with you, things will appear different. Doing good starts with taking care of yourself and giving yourself the much needed time! Spare some time from your hectic routine and get a grasp of your thoughts. You need to communicate with yourself in order to know what is going on in your mind. Once you know, you can streamline the things for the better.

The next step is to open your mind to anything that comes to you. An open mindset will allow you to see things from a new perspective which was hindered by your closed mindset. This entails that you must stop resistance to new ideas. Be cautious towards what others have to say and consider the thoughts and suggestions given to you by others.

This concept of thinking is further intensified by saying that you need to forget the past events, especially those that bring pain to you. You need to learn to let go of things as this will enable you to oversee the pinching elements of your life and see it from a whole new perspective.

It is often the undesired events that turn you to a bitter personality. The thinking process is the thing affected initially and you change your mind into a somewhat 'negative magnet.' As your mind is a powerful magnet which channelizes the energies around you, this negative magnet attracts more negativity into your life and you are left in despair – you feel life has ended and you can't do anything about it. You start feeling as a useless person present on the face of earth and you don't want to face the challenges life has thrown on you. The negative repute surrounds you and you feel extremely helpless. If you reach this stage, then it's high time you consider revising your personality. Change your thinking by negating any negative thoughts, comments and force yourself to see the good in everything that comes to you. Remember – it's not a half empty glass; it's a glass half full!

Reinvented thinking will help you revive. You are nothing but a mere collection of your thoughts. When you have got hold of your mind, you have won half the game! You are now the rider of your thoughts and as you are committed to seeing the good in everything, good starts coming to you. You feel reinvented and this is something that is actually important.

Always look at the positive side of your life. Kick out the negative thoughts. Your negativity will try to resist you by saying nothing is happening. Throw these thoughts out. Assure yourself that even if nothing happens, you are not going to lose anything. Think that earthquakes destroy everything in seconds, but it takes a long period to revive and certainly doesn't mean revival should not take place.

Your thinking should be focused on relaxing you, not tiring you up. Do not punish yourself for your previous follies. Appreciate the fact that you are human and all humans make mistakes. If something went wrong previously, don't blame yourself because you think it was your fault, think of it as something that didn't work. Focus on finding new ways of making it work, instead of beating about the one that did not work. Thinking of finding new ways will not only shift your focus from negative thoughts to a fresh new aspect, it will also provide you to do something new and therefore, move forward with it.

If you give it a thought, this process automatically revives the creativity that you once had, and brings back the zeal of working hard to achieve your new thoughts and ideas. In practice, this process will be easier said than done. It is human psychology to live in the paradigm that we are in and do not wish to change, other things remaining the same. It is true of negativity in that once we tend to get the hang of it; we do not want to leave it. Your negativity will also resist in every manner, but be brave. Take a bold step against it. Remember, it is the first drop of rain that is the most courageous to jump towards the earth, and the rest follow suit. When you get up to throw out your negativity, the rest of your senses and suppressed emotions will soon follow. When your heart knows that you are feeling good, you will be automatically inclined towards celebrating your good choices and this process will give you a boost.

To back up the whole concept, it is not the perfect person that satisfies us the most, it is that learning to see the perfection in the imperfections that changes the whole story – and obviously that is what is brought to you by positive thinking!

Do You Know How Habits Are Formed ?

Now that you have left all the negativity behind, have jumped out of your discouraging thoughts, are suggesting the good to yourself and are empowered with a boost of positive energy, you are all ready to set your objectives and self-goals.

You need to define your goals from getting up in the morning to earning money to taking out time to hang out with your friends. Remind yourself never to overwork or over-burden or you will miss many important moments of life. Neither do you need to spend all your time working, nor do you have to party all the time. Remember, balance is the key to success! And to incorporate that balance, you have to set a goal that allows you to empower yourself and let you succeed. Balanced goals enable you to enjoy every aspect of life while staying true to your ultimate cause. These provide you with the required elements of fun, passion, zeal and work that drives your personality. Thus, your personality speaks loud of your balanced approach and you enter the success zone with a vivid enthusiasm.

As you are empowered, you have the desired ability of controlling your life and its purpose. Your aptitude defines your objectives and your self-esteem gets developed to a level that it settles for no less than you actually deserve. You now know what you are capable of and what you deserve. Thus, you become clear regarding your objectives and tend to stay away from all those possibilities that can bring you down. This is because you are focused on your goals and want to attain them at any cost.

The process of establishing goals starts with the fulfillment of the basic needs. You must realize the fact that unless your basic needs are catered for, your need of a superior level can't be satisfied. Basic needs include your essentials and when you entail those basics, you tend to have a satisfactory stance which motivates you to move towards an enhanced lifestyle. This is the stage where you need to recognize that there are social goals which then need to be attained.

Social goals must be approached with a prepared and a content mindset. This is because you are getting out of your negative stance and shedding your negative repute as well. Start building good terms with people around you. Ensure that you are not considered an outcast and perfectly suit the interactions taking place. These actions will make you appear acceptable to the society and people will want to interact more with you. This is only because in you they see a highly organized person who is committed to his/her goals and is accomplishing the defined objectives as he/she desired. Thus, you become the center of focus for all and yes, you have been successful in gathering people around you. You have a good repute and are being praised for your positive attributes. Your long lost dream is coming true and hence, the relationship between your goals and the ultimate objective proves itself and you have effectively hitched your wagon to success.

Remember that the interaction with yourself and others decide your future and these are defined by the goals you have determined to achieve. Your personal self is very important and must be cared for the most in order to get you on the road to success. It would be a good idea to include an exercise schedule as this will refresh your brain and help you exhale all the detoxifications. Sparing some time for the community is also a very positive step towards building your personality. All that you have become must be imparted to others as well. Moreover, remember the schema 'the good you do comes back to you.' Therefore, doing good to others must be a part of the greater goals that surround you. The good will come back to make you stronger and thus, the world see you emerge as a smarter, stronger and better person.

Brace Your Subconscious For Success

Now that your thinking is on the right path, it's time to take it to a whole new level. After good thinking, comes the stage where you use your thinking to your own benefit. The way by which you achieve this is called 'the art of suggestion'.

Suggestion is defined as the process by which one manifests the power of the energies around him/her and puts it to a good use so as to get things done. Scientifically speaking, suggestion is the process of programming the subconscious part of the mind in order to influence the operations of the conscious mind. If done correctly, this can have a big impact upon your thinking as well as your overall living. If done consistently over a period of time, suggestion can harvest unimaginable achievements for a person; the only thing it can't conquer is death. Therefore it is high time that you use the power of suggestion to completely transform your life. Here is what you need to do.

The science behind suggestions is what you would want to think, not what you should think under the given circumstances. Here is an example where you imagine yourself sitting in a boat in the midst of a sea. Conventional thinking is what would happen to you if you only predict where the currents would take you under the pertinent conditions of wind, current speed and boat direction without taking any action on your part. Suggestion, in this context, would be to plan your route, take action by rowing the boat, lifting the masts or steering it so as to take it to a dry piece of land, where you want to be.

Now let us focus on to you. You want to shed your negative reputation. You want to get rid of your negative stance on life. You want to be extremely successful with both life and people. To begin with, focus on your thinking process that you have transformed and be happy that you have reached so far. You now need to increase your levels of concentration. For this, spare yourself sometime between 9'o o'clock and midnight. Choose a lightly lit and quite corner where there is least chance of hindrance. Sit on the floor with legs crossed. Keep your spine in a straight and upright position; it should not be bent. Relax your arms, close your eyes and take a deep breath. Hold your breath for five seconds and then exhale very slowly. Start with five minutes daily and add thirty seconds every day until you reach half an hour. Make sure that you inhale through your nose and exhale through your mouth. After this exercise, your head will feel light, empty and calm. Now you have cleared your brain of all thoughts and are ready to take up what you 'suggest to it'. So go straight to your bed and prepare to sleep. When you are in this state of half sleep, half awake, say out to yourself 'I am becoming positive' or say 'I am becoming more positive by the day'. Say it to yourself five to ten times and then go to sleep straight away. When you rise up in the morning and are again half asleep, half awake, suggest the same lines to yourself.

Of course, some of your negative perception that might be left will tell you that it is good for nothing, useless exercise that yields nothing. Kick out such thoughts immediately even if nothing is happening. Surprisingly, you will see over a period of ten to fifteen days that there are drastic changes in your thinking, mood, way of looking at life and interactions with others. By this time, your subconscious mind would have manifested the good energies around you to bring about a positive change.

You can also devise similar suggestions for health and wealth like 'I am losing illnesses and becoming stronger' or 'More money each day, everyday'. This might sound imaginative but you must believe that it works. Give it a try and you will know – you will reap its fruits. Even the sensation of this is so enjoyable. Imagine yourself where people adore you, enjoy the feeling of being adored, empowered and admired for the charismatic positivity. Plant these feelings of success and wellbeing in your brain. It is a pot of positivity that you are planting in your brain; it will one day grow into a tall, strong and fruitful tree of health, wealth, positivity and success.

When you only suggest the good to yourself, you have committed to see the good in everything and thereby, you cumulate the positive energies around you. Your life turns into a series of beautiful events and you are surprised by the results. When you tend to think over matters, it is only your perception which has changed and all of this is turning into a reality because you said NO to any negativity and have closed all the pathways that could lead to negativity.

However, you must remember that the 'art of suggestion' is similar to muscle building. You stay in shape till you practice, and lose it as soon as you stop practicing. That being said, you need to continue suggesting yourself for a fairly long period of time; provided you have just stepped out of the negative phase of your life. Obviously, you will reach a maturity level where you wouldn't need any sort of suggestions but that will be when you are strong enough to empower your brain and retain the positive energies. Carry on knowing how you would empower yourself and achieve the much needed success in your life.

Become a thought leader and master your success. Growing up is a detailed process which incorporates a lot of complexities of life. It includes the formation of your physical, as well as your mental and emotional being. Though you are born with the natural abilities of thinking rationally and logically about everything that takes place in your life, you often tend to ignore your natural tendencies and take a deep impact of anything that is just not according to your will. Remember that there is a difference in what you perceive to be is right and what is actually right. When things do not turn out the way you want, negativity pops in!

Also when you grow up, you build your perceptions and set of beliefs. These define your thoughts and you buy in anything that matches your perceptions and negate anything that is just not at your accord. You often tend to skip some of the most important details of life in the process. Those details are often the most important ones and it is that *skipping* which converts you into a negative person you are today. That negativity not only has an overall negative impact on your basic life, but also leads you towards everything that is negative in itself – this is because you perceive yourself as a misfit in the positives. Thus, you tend to get involved in things that are right according to your belief system and start building your repute. As the growing process involves routine interactions, you tend to engage in negative activities which apparently tend to satisfy your mental stance. Negative repute jumps into your life as soon as you socialize with those around you as they can see the negativity pop out from you. People rather start repelling you and you are left with little logic as to why they are doing so. And as you are in such a negative stance, you are unable to come up with rational thoughts regarding your behavior as well as of those surrounding you. You try to hitch your wagon to them, but receive rejection. This further intensifies the negativity in you and you are nothing more than a cluster of negativity. Very soon you find yourself as someone with a negative repute and try to look out for ways that can help you come out of the negativity and turn you back into a person you once were – and this is the most desired of all life pleasures!

The process of turning back into a positive person, your innate persona starts right now. Before you waste any time understanding life and what it has thrown on you, you need to push and fill yourself with an ambition which not only enables you to combat the negative reputation you have built, but acts as a guide towards the greater goals of life. Only when you have built a mindset that is only committed to seeing the positivity in everything, you can really change your life and to this world!

The more you become this, the more you'll have success. Until now, we have learned that you might be stuck in a negative life and what you need is a revival. The revival starts with your thinking process and goes on to the art of suggesting. For now, you need to adhere to the fact that what required of you is empowerment, so let's now discover the concept.

Empowerment is strongly linked to self-boosting and the confidence which you acquire as you live your life. You are not born empowered, but you learn it along the way. However, encountering several incidents in life makes you lose all the power you have gained so far and this marks the beginning of your negativity. Reviving often takes time, but the hardest part is to realize that you actually need to revive. Acceptance is important and as soon as you realize that nobody is perfect, things get easier. You then need to sort things out and establish where you have been lacking.

It is an incontestable fact that gathering the courage and confidence boosts you and allows you to face the challenges life has thrown on you. The fear you face and the things that demoralize you shatters your confidence and you start to entail a negative perception. The worst part is that you start thinking that you can't do anything. This 'can't' is something which makes things fall apart. Never let anyone dictate you that you can't. Tell yourself you can and start working towards your objectives. Telling yourself you can will empower you from within. It is your life, and your will should rule it. But first you need to gather all your powers within and execute them with vigor. Once you are headed towards attracting the positive powers and channelizing those around you, you are on your way to prove the cynics wrong.

Another tactic for empowering is to tell yourself there is no boundary to your imagination. Imagine as far as you can, and beyond! It is the power of your imagination that will take you to your intended success. The sky is yours and your sky knows no bounds! Think to the extreme of your imagination and bring determination into action. When your imagination is coupled with thinking and determination, you are sure to realize it and soon you experience an amazing reality coming into being.

Remember that empowering is a self-building tool which if rightly used will nourish your life. A further step towards breaking into power is to crack any sealing that is bringing you down. You need to stay away from all the negative people and if you had previously been pleasing people, you need to start right away. It is essential because these habits do not allow you to grow and you cannot use your power as a self-building tool.

Empowerment comes from experience. You need to turn your experiences into learning which gives you valuable insight into life matters. As you tend to look at experiences as a means of giving lessons, you change your mental perceptions and try to look at the positive things in life. This act of learning empowers you which enhance your outlook and overall personality. You therefore entail value and see beyond the apparent scenario. Thus, whomever you meet or come across, you have an inherent stance of learning this is the basic element which empowers your personality.

You need to realize the need to be completely honest with yourself and define the purpose of your life. It is your purpose which will define your direction. But before you have your purpose defined, tell yourself that you need to dream big. Your dreams must be evocative of your passion and unless you are passionate about converting your life into a powerful stream of happiness, you cannot land onto the happy-land.

Once you have determined and started your journey towards empowerment, you need to get going. Though you might face some setbacks along your way, but ensure that your determination will not allow you to stop unless you have achieved what you intended to. Give yourself a reminder that such setbacks are a part of the process and you have to face them with courage. Likewise, do not get swayed by the successes – they must not stop you from achieving better.

During the process, you need to show gratitude as this helps you open up to your surroundings. Courteousness is an important aspect that comes in with empowerment. When you are thankful for what you have, you instill a sense of satisfaction which nourishes your spirit. You then tend to make the best use of what you have as you value it to the best of your abilities. Your hidden abilities which you had almost forgotten will take you to the next level, putting your energies to effective and positive use, further empowering you.

The best part of empowering is that your empowered personality becomes a source for empowering others. People start gathering around you just because they like to be with you. The ultimate dilemma you were facing with the negative repute was that people had started to avoid you and there was little that you were able to do in that regard. The good news is that now you are in a position to take definite measures and not only influence the people surrounding you, but also empower them with your thoughts.

With empowerment comes self-realization which allows you to carry yourself with a vigor and energy. People start getting impressed from your personality as your personality now is depictive of someone who carries himself/herself in a very decent manner. Your personality emits the powerful vibes that are capable to attract others and influence them for the better. The issue of your life is resolved that had been hampering your way to success.

Most people would like more money. Some people try to accomplish this by saving as much as they possibly can. They practice frugality, clip coupons, and buy in bulk. And there's nothing wrong with that. But... no one gets RICH just by being frugal!

If you want to have financial freedom and the ability to live the kind of life you dream about, there's no way around it: you have to make more money. So as we near the end of 2019, we would like to help you create a solid plan to create more wealth in 2020.

Try visualizing this. You have a business and you make money on the amount of people who sign up through you. The bigger the network, the greater the profits.

You become an independent business owner and run it from your house or any place of your liking.

You continue living the life you always dreamt of living, and take care of yourself and your loved ones.

You help people do the same and what can be more rewarding?

The network grows and you continue getting the profits while others earn from it too.

You play your part in helping others live the life they deserve and suddenly you become a better citizen.

Ah, this sounds so good, doesn't it?

This all is possible and doable, but through persistence and consistency. Are you ready for it? Let's do this. Together. For the better.

Learn How to Save Money Now in Order to Invest in a More Financially Secure Future!

The internet these days is full of saving advice. Podcasts, bestselling books and what not, but most often, we tend to overlook people around us who might have the best advice. People share what works best for them on various forums which have been compiled for your rescue. To help you secure your future, some of the best money saving tips are here.

- When going grocery shopping, never go hungry. It has been found that you tend to overspend on items you don't need when you go shopping hungry.

- Try delaying a purchase for a couple of weeks. This way, you'll know whether you really want it or not. If you still need it after two weeks, go get it.
- Always save the change. It might seem like a small amount but you will be surprised to see the sum when you count it after a month.

- Plan in advance and wait for the sales. A lot of sales take place after the holidays that you can use to your advantage. When you've things written down and planned, you can do the up-coming season's shopping from sales. This might mean you will have to buy after your holidays but hey, you've got the next season planned. Do the same with your decorations, Christmas accessories and any gifts you want for your loved ones.

- Try cooking at home and curtail your outings. Not only has it had a massively positive impact on your health but your budget as well. You might end up surprising yourself for the money you saved, and yeah, you can then treat yourself – a budget and health friendly advice.

- When buying an item, remember to convert the price into your hourly wage rate. Ask yourself: is the product worth the hours you spent? There you got your answer.

- Calculate your savings and transfer the saved amount to your savings account. Although it might not be a lot, it will add up at the end of the year.

- Skipping soda and other drinks on a daily basis can help you save above 100 bucks every month. You didn't see that coming!

- Avoid impulse purchases as you might want to rethink whether you want something or not. Planning your purchases can help you in this regard. Another useful tactic is to have a separate savings account so you can give yourself the time to think before buying.

- Try to do your shopping when the companies have promo codes running. You will save yourself a few bucks and get your most favorite thing at a good price.
- Plan your kitchen menu in accordance with the promotions on groceries. Eat whatever is on sale and voila, you've got some extra money on your hands to save.

These little tips will help you live your life in a well-planned manner. A few changes here and there and you can save money you never thought of saving. Use this money to make small investments and secure your future. Not to forget, you can utilize these savings over the years to invest in real estate. Remember, that is the real asset you will have. Such savings will also generate returns for you in the long run and you're good to go!

Did You Get High On Self-Enhancement? You Need To Constantly Evolve!

Behavior or your set of actions collectively makes up your personality – a personality which defines how you will be treated. While you go through the process of turning yourself into a better person , you are basically enhancing your personality. The thinking process, the art of suggesting, empowerment and the setting of objectives are all that have been shaping your personality. This adheres to the fact that behavioral change is a must if you want to succeed – and not just a behavioral change, but a positive behavioral change.

You need to focus strongly on your overall behavior in view of striving to become better. This entails that you need to be mindful of your implicit and explicit behaviors. Implicit behavior includes your natural aptitude towards the surroundings. Though your life experiences would have been shaping your tastes and preferences up till now, you need to be mindful of your aptitude in order to stay away from everything you have just considered bad for you. These would include negative behavior patterns, negative thoughts when any event came up as well as feeling helpless. Your psychology also forms part of the implicitness and you have to be wary of it! Every single thought that crosses your mind is reflected in your words, gestures and actions and you have to be cautious. Don't try to think that you can hide the nature of thoughts you are having. You might be able to hide what you have been thinking, but you cannot hide the good or bad that is in you – that comes to you naturally, and thus, forms part of your implicit behavior. It therefore becomes very important that everything you think of is positive nature so you can emit the positivity while roaming around!

The explicit behavior patterns are the patterns adopted consciously and deliberately as a means of enhancing your outlook. Though your implicit personality has a deep connection with your explicit ones and your natural inclination for the explicit behavior is towards your implicit preferences. Your explicit behavior thus is deeply affected by your inherent fondness and you define your comfort zone with a combination of implicit and explicit behaviors. This pertains to be the reason why we feel comfortable with a specific group of people rather than everyone.

It's also important to note that it is your behavior which determines your social standing. Whether you like to be with someone or whether someone likes to be with you is highly dependent upon how your implicit and explicit likeness treats them. For instance, you see someone who is wearing your favorite brand. You develop a natural liking for that person, due to your inherent mindset, but at a conscious level. Hence, your behavior appears to be a collection of your implicit and explicit personality. Whether you feel uncomfortable around a certain group of people is also determined by your mind and will shape your behavior.

You must try to gauge where your behavior is leading you. In the process, you will come across several factors that will determine how you react to each of them. You might be reactive in situations that are unfavorable and you react pleasantly to things which are according to your will. Watch out for anything that is bringing you down and immediately eliminate it from your life. When you do so, you are making sure that your future behavior is not guided by any factor that can make things worse for you. Moreover, stay away from any such thing in the future and be careful. What sort of person you become and you are perceived is solely determined by how you behave. Thereby, you have to behave in the best possible manner at all times, give the best to life and let life give the best to you. You must be the sole determinant of your behavior! Do NOT let others lead you. Be your own leader and see the results. You have to be practically the best person that you can be and show others that it's actually possible!

Remember, it is your behavior which signals out to others as to how you ought to be treated. It thus needs to be considerate of your passion, ego and must not compromise your self-respect at any cost. Your self-respect is the most important thing and has to be a part of your behavior. Unless you respect yourself, others will not! Therefore, respect yourself in order to get respect. Also be very humble and polite in your dealings. Give respect, get respect! When you are good to others, others will be good to you. However, never compromise your self being in the course. Do as much good you can while considering your limits. The good you are doing must not cause you trouble because after all, you can only give the best when you retain your perfect stance.

Can You Feel Better By Just Doing Nothing? Practice Motivation!

As of now, we have learned about the behavior patterns we need to keep up with in order to count amongst the good personalities around, next we need to know how to carry on with the same zeal, passion and energy.

Retaining your positive stance for a temporary period of time is quite easy – but what is difficult is to carry along with the same energy for a lifetime. This fact might drown you for a moment but hey, that is not difficult than your initial build up phase. If you can combat your negative stance so easily, coping up along is straightforward.

The art of keeping up or motivation is the element that is required to fill you with the much-needed boost of passion to get you going. It not only provides you with a purpose for struggling for the better, but also provides you with a sense of recognition. Yes, now is the time you consciously recognize yourself and take action to maintain your identity. What is important is that your mind realizes your importance, your potential and is ready to give you a reason to perform better.

So basically, what is motivation? Motivation is the art that inculcates positive behavior in you and provides you with the zest you need to achieve your goals. It is what triggers you to take the action – whether it is as small as reading a book or as big as accomplishing your dream! It provides the reason to your rational thinking process as to why you are doing something. Note that it can be as small as wanting to get good grades, or as big as shedding your negative repute.

It is motivation which provides you with the reason to act and determines the intensity of the chosen action. Often you find yourself least bothered to even stick to your daily chores. This happens because you don't have enough reason to do them. You need reasons, and very compelling ones to convert your thoughts into practical actions. And before you can take any action, it is often the motivation that inspires you enough.

Having your goals ahead of you, you need to achieve them with a constant and never ending passion. Motivation sprouts it within you and you are ready to face all the obstacles and endure all the difficulties just to achieve your goals. This is the trait of successful people who are motivated enough to conquer the world. Now look around you, think about the names that emerge on the big screen. All of them have stayed true to their cause and have used their motivation to achieve what they desired. This proves that even you can achieve what you desire. All that you need is the right insight with a pinch of passion to get you going.

Everything you have learned up till now suddenly interlinks itself. None of the elements you have learned work in isolation. Everything is connected to the other and must be carried on along in order to bring effective results. For instance, you can't expect to exhibit good behavior without having a strong reason to do so. This reason can't come to you unless you have a clear and empowered mind; and you can't have an empowered mind unless you are committed to good and positive thinking. One of the elements goes missing and the whole process is disrupted. So yes, everything happens to take a cyclical approach and the process repeats over and over again.

This Will Make Your Success Inevitable – Connect With Successful People

Energetic individuals, motivated entrepreneurs and amazing marketers, these characteristics should introduce you wherever you go.

Successful people have a lot in common. They are empathic, with a motive of serving humanity. They want to build their lives around things they are passionate about, and that's how they go about it – they take charge of their lives and help others succeed. They think of possibilities that would help them get partners in everything they do. They build partnerships for better opportunities!

Being blessed with everything you ever imagined, you need to push yourself beyond the boundaries. Take one step at a time and everything else will just settle. Successful people help you do what you really want to do. They want you to develop the abilities God has given you and listen to your true calling. Do you know how you can entail success?

Understanding your motive of being here, we are now just about to unveil the secret recipe of success – networking. Networking is everything. It is like a well-oiled machine that communicates and engages to create a dynamic lifestyle. However, this apparently small recognition has taken years of research.

It was in lieu of this that we seriously studied the multi-billionaires and millionaire entrepreneurs and examined their secrets of success. One thing that appeared to be common amongst all is their networking – their businesses were all an amalgamation of personal attributes.

Our research enabled us to formulate a model that is focused on the wellness of others. It appears that when you collaborate and connect with others, you develop insurmountable synergies. You look for solutions that enable everyone to win.

Understanding the diversity and richness of life, you ought to come to terms with the fact that everybody needs some positive force to explore their inner self. This also includes their principles and the need to boost their psychological performance. Successful people are that force for each other, but again, not everybody is as lucky as it seems. They work for it and get it. You can too!

We want everyone to be the shining star of their lives. Discovering the secret recipe of success, we have been implementing this in our lives. But what good is life if we are not able to help others succeed along ourselves? This is why we have a special mission of helping every individual around us to recognize his/her true calling.

Passion and a thirst for learning is what helps one discover the purpose of life and enables one to perform splendidly. Understanding that not everybody might be privileged enough to apprehend the road to success, this book will help you get what you have always wanted to achieve.

What this book will actually help you to do?

Our main mission is to help you develop a lifestyle that would enable you to enjoy with your families. Everyone wants to live a life as smooth and peaceful as it can get – away from the chaos of 9-5 routine, succumbing to the tantrums of bosses and making JUST enough to pay the bills. Obviously you are not here to pay the bills ONLY. There's much more to life and it is your right to explore your true potential.

Life will often give you a flashback of how everything was planned in a divine manner. Everything was perfectly aligned with your life's purpose, and how it enables you to cater to a growing number of people around you. Nothing can be more fulfilling and soothing.

Everyone wants partners who would support them in everything they do. We all need someone who is understanding and cooperative enough to recognize our real potential and promote our growth. And that's why we need to network with the successful lot.

It is this primary need that should motivate you to become a better version of yourselves. Only when you are able to love yourselves enough, can you serve the needs of others.

The primary motive of this book is to let you live to your truest potential by understanding the success and live a better life. Who doesn't want a life filled with abundance and richness? Well, millionaires have been living it and you can live it as well.

Anything is possible if you believe it enough. It's all in the mind, and all you need is to empower it. Experience it firsthand; do not let your mind control you. Rather, be the one controlling it. This has enabled many to jump heaps of uncertainty while winning it every time.

How to create the best day of your life day after dayHaving learnt about everything you need to make your life a successful one, you must now settle with your inner self. The prime reason as to why you were in trouble was that your inner self was at conflict with your outer self. And as you were not being able to figure out the reasons, you were unable to find peace.

Now that you have figured out what needs to be done and what needs to be corrected, you first need to forgive yourself for not being at peace. Only when you have accepted this fact can you move ahead. Surrender yourself to your condition and start finding peace – it will now naturally come to you. The problem exists because you don't want to accept it. As things have soothed out and you have experienced them turning your way, your mind and body is somewhat relaxed. You now tend to be more open to things and look at the broader picture.

Remember, peace is something that comes from within, and thus, as stated earlier, you need to spare some time for yourself. You need to sit in a quiet place, stop all sorts of thoughts and detach yourself from the rest of the world – what should remain is only YOU! This will permit you to feel the goodness coming to you! This will also enable you to focus on the things good life has brought and the millions of blessings you have been ignoring up till now.

Finding peace will allow you to look at the brighter side of life – the prevalent good in the world. You will come to realize that the same world has much more than you were able to see before. There is a lot which you can give to this world and a lot that you can absorb. Remember, it's always your perception about things that makes it good or bad. Thus, change your perception and look out for peace. As a last resort, stop expecting from others.

Be grateful, show gratitude, be happy and be content. Only when you are at your best, can you give the best to this world! Give life your best hit and don't worry about the results. The peace you actually entail within is what matters the most. Everything else is only a part of the journey – your journey, so make sure it is worth living!

The Truth About Successful Persons

Financially successful people have a long term vision which enables them to see beyond the horizon. Collection of information about the financial affairs, nature and capabilities of entities of interest is referred to as financial intelligence. It also goes on to depict their future actions and intentions. Knowing the term, it now becomes easy to understand how it goes on to cover the area of financial success.

So, are you ready for retirement? Value investing can help!

Before you reach your retirement, you must ensure you have sufficient funds that will help you with your day to day expenses. One way to consider this is to know whether your savings are giving a fulfilling rate of return. But ever wondered how will you earn better returns? This calls for planning and here comes 3D value investing as a savior in the darkest hour!

Talking about value investing, Warren Buffett comes to mind who has given a new meaning to the term. He has appeared as one of the biggest value investors and reflecting his genius in his investment plans, he explains why you can earn great returns too and prepare for a better future.

The concept revolves around purchasing stocks which are traded at discounted values based on a fundamental analysis, which will bring higher profits in the future. The reason is that these stocks are undervalued by the market, and traded on less than their intrinsic value.

3D value investing is about hitting the best possible targets by applying some rules that will help earn a handsome return. These rules help in the minimization of risk in your investment. All you need to do is consider the amount of return you expect your target company to earn. Return on equity will be a helpful ratio in this regard. Next, you can use the past trends in profit margins to predict future returns and then using the debt to equity ratio, you can consider how much you and other holders of equity will benefit from the growth of the company.

These indicators, as used by Buffett can aid in selecting the right stocks in terms of the value the stocks entail. Have you been worrying about your life after retirement? You don't need to panic now. Just plan your life using the right insight and it will bring you the same benefits it has brought to the other successful investors! Give it a try! Develop the rich habits and you will never have to worry.

Rich Habits vs. Poor Habits

Busting out the myths here, you need to understand that rich habits are the only reason successful people are rich. Over the years, many people have formulated some myths which have succeeded in brainwashing the layman who would have otherwise worked towards becoming successful. So in this section, we will burst the bubble for you and help you ascertain for yourself the difference between rich habits and poor habits.

Myth # 1 – Rich people are lucky

Anyone who is unsuccessful would like to believe that the successful people have a good luck all along. They tend to build an argument that it is good luck that brings you success. While this is true to some extent, no one ever got lucky just by sitting and doing nothing. The random good or bad luck is something you have no control over. Anything that brings random luck, whether good or bad, is out of your control and you can do nothing about it. But good luck, that brings opportunity, is a result of your consistent habits that help you succeed on a daily basis. This is like preparing the garden, planting the seeds and nurturing them until they grow and bear fruit. This fruit happens to be the result of daily small steps you continue to do over a long duration. It is this fruit that represents the opportunity you have been presented with.

Successful people do the things that are imperative for growth and sustenance in the long run. They start living the rich habits every single day. Mind you, it is these habits that that attract good luck. Much of this is unexpected, and can be inferred as the law of attraction. People who live the rich habits attract opportunities in lieu of law of attraction.

Likewise, unsuccessful people live the bad habits that bring them detrimental luck. Serving as the evil twin of opportunity luck, detrimental luck has its roots in the bad habits that people live every day. This is what brings bad luck to unsuccessful people because they fail to formulate a healthy pattern in their daily routine.

Now that you know, you ought to have the right luck by attracting it. Living the rich habits daily, you will attract the right luck.

Myth # 2 – Rich people inherit their wealth

Research has found that 60-70 percent of millionaires are self-made (Dougherty, 2013). These are the people who created their rich reality. They don't inherit their wealth – they work for it; they create it.

Myth # 3 – Rich people have it easy

Little do the people know that rich people who've become millionaires work far more than everyone else? Following a rigorous routine that makes them stand out from the crowd, the self-made people have many more working hours than a layman. The Census Bureau reported that an average wealthy person worked five times more than an average poor person on a daily basis. Isn't it enough proof that the rich work harder than everyone else? Yes, but this is not a hard and fast rule. They tend to have a better work ethic. The rich work harder because they are very passionate about what they do. It is this passion that results in the devotion of a greater number of hours. It is unfortunate that many people don't like what they do for a living which is why they just keep the cycle going without going the extra mile.

However, when we talk about the ultra-rich, having a net worth of $5million or more, work is taken on a different realm. Richard Branson, owner of Virgin Atlantic and Virgin Airlines along with 20 other companies, works for 12-14 hours a day. He explains that he loves what he does and he loves the people he works with. So if someone had to play for 12-14 hours a day, would you call him a hard worker?

Nonetheless, the uber-rich do not work as per the society's definition of work. They are extremely passionate about what they do. When you do something you want to do, you are not working. It no longer remains work. It becomes fun – and who wouldn't want to have fun for 14 hours daily?

Myth 4 – Rich people are better educated

If you were to study the wealthiest people of the world, you'll know that almost half of them never went to university. There are even a few who did not even complete their primary school; Andrew Carnegie being a prime example. The ground reality is that the rich people make the most out of what they have on their plate. They didn't start out better or smarter, but they took that opportunity at hand and adopted habits that made them successful.

The rich habits

As described earlier, habits pertain to be unconscious behavior that comprises of thinking and emotions.

Part 2

Millionaire Habits – Is It A Mindset?

Are you in a situation that calls for some immediate action? You've wondered and wondered, and luckily, you have concluded that in order to be the ultimate controller of your life, you need to change your mindset. You've just started to research it. It has dawned on you that entailing an abundance mindset can help one attain great heights. What's needed is a sharp razor focus.

This simple shift in the mindset is a dangerous thing – the only thing stopping one from having more money and happiness is their own mindset. Once you start to practice having the right mindset, you become addicted to it.

You will literally enjoy life like never before. Never in your wildest imaginations have you thought of experiencing everything the way you have planned. You will start to have control over your life, your finances, spend time with your family and most importantly, you will feel happy. The happiness that you thought was lost long ago will be regained.

As of now, we are avid believer of the concept that having the right mindset is everything for having a great successful life. That said, we want you to be successful. If Richard Brunson can do it, so can you. Now you might be wondering why are we so interested in leveraging your life. Well, the fact remains that the biggest happiness comes when people transform their lives, both financial and personal. When you follow these secrets hidden in this book, you will experience this shift for yourself. And because it is a trait of the highly unsuccessful to keep whining but when given the opportunity to take charge of their lives, they back off.

Success Is The Only Path That Matters

Are you seeking professional help for developing the right mindset? Have you exhausted the resources at hand and are still clueless? Developing the rich mindset is imperative for your growth, or you will be stuck in your current reality forever.

But didn't you just think that the rich people had it easy? An outright no is the answer. The rich and successful help people upgrade their life through developing income streams. They talk about how to get clarity of your true calling – or how to enhance your life to the next level. Basically, they talk about how to make a living doing what you love. The key is to know how to decode your life – decode everything that is hidden in your life story so you can entail success.

We are very serious when we say that your protective patterns are sabotaging your success. Don't get us wrong, but there are things sabotaging your success. What we are going to tell you will heal a lifetime of struggle. Not only it will give you so much momentum, it will give you the power to break out your boundaries. When we talk about boundaries, it includes fear, overwhelming desires and procrastination that's holding you back.

We can help you with this in very little time. We want to share how this works, and why this is doable. We want you to know that it's one of the most transformational quantum leaps you may have ever had – including coaching, mentoring, and healing all in one. There's one reality of life that the rich learnt the hard way. The reality is that a person only lives the same year every year of his/her life, but the protective patterns remain the same.

They are no different. They kept living the same life and didn't know of any way that would enable them to jump out of their comfort zone. They try hard, and after stumbling upon a lot of options, they finally found the key to their financial freedom: investing and reinvesting.

Are you an entrepreneur? A small business owner? Are you adventurous? Are you an adrenaline junkie? Do you need passive income or an additional income stream?

If you answered yes to any of the questions above, this will help you build income streams that will be a game changer for you.

While many of you think that it's very late to make a career change, it's not. It's never too late – whether you're in your 20s, 30s, 40s, 50s or 60s. As long as you are alive, you have the chance to make your life better – and you deserve a better life no matter what.

Just to start, you need to think about which of your actions are limiting your right to an enhanced life and which of your beliefs are adding to it? Have you ever asked yourself this question: where do you want your life to head? Where do you want to see yourself later in life?

All the people who you think are sorted out didn't start like that. They didn't have the direction that led towards success. They were unaware where their life was directed. One day, it suddenly occurred to them that this was a limiting belief and if they wanted to succeed, they needed to overcome that.

Unlike you, they have realized that it was this belief that was keeping them from moving forward in their life. At first, the now rich were in grave shock to know the answer to a lifelong question: why can't they make the impact they want?

They came to realize that they never tried to come out of their comfort zone, which was keeping them away from growing into the person they always wanted to be.

All of a sudden, they were into a new stance – a shift of mindset. Experiencing a mindset shift is like questioning anything and everything that would hinder your growth. Consequently, the people you now deem as successful and rich changed their whole belief system which enhanced their life all in all.

Now, we have a question for you. Is 2019 everything you thought it would be so far? Are you finding it easy to enhance your life? Do you have a clear path to your financial freedom?

This book is your answer – a place where you will learn all about how to enhance your life and how to live the way you want.

We are sure that you like exploring new places and people as much as everyone else. We also know that you want to learn new stuff but can't because of financial constraints. The good news is that it's all possible if you give yourself the much needed financial freedom.

You need to keep everything at bay that's blocking your success. You need to manifest your truest potential so you can experience the life you deserve.

Here's the good news. We have got something that will change your life forever. Here's a small token of advice for you.

Find beauty in everyday whether in the people around you or somewhere in creation. Sometimes it is harder than other times but keep on searching. You will find it! And when you find it, don't ever let it go.

Implement the learning now and you'll understand what's going on in your life. You need to break your barriers and let go of the negative forces in your life. You will learn that you can take a back seat and still enjoy all the good life has to offer.

You Should Know This

How would you describe your personality and how you ought to differ from those who you deem as rich and powerful? You know there are some traits in people which make them rich and successful. Are you a caring and compassionate person who is driven by contribution? Do you know what makes people rich and wealthy?

They want to contribute something positive to this world. They pertain to have a positive mindset that attracts wellness for them. They think that life has given them so much goodness and so, they remain indebted to it and want to contribute something to the world so they can live in peace. It is something they perceive as their duty towards others.

Like everyone, don't you want to control your time and money? Well, who doesn't want that? Obviously, you do. Spending a great life themselves, the successful want everyone else to do the same. This is why they reveal how they got there; this is what they strive for: to give people a life that they can control.

Being the sole controller of one's life is the only road to success which is why we are trying to help you move from the left side (Employee & Self-employed) of Robert Kiyosaki's CashFlow Quadrant to the right side (Business Owner & Investor).

Also remember that building multiple income streams is purely a trait of the millionaires. They never rely on a single source of income. Haven't you heard never put all your eggs in a single basket? As such, it is imperative that you take charge of your life and build passive income. You need to develop income strategies that replace job income. Remember, this income will be there every month, without you having to show up and work for it.

The rich and successful are also business enthusiasts. They motivate people to hustle and build real businesses. You can work part-time to grow your business and continue to provide income even through retirement.

Whether you are a male or female, married or single, looking after a family or not, income strategies of the rich suit all. Everyone struggles through building a lifestyle they imagined. The rich do too: the urge to build a lifestyle one has always imagined but not being able to convert that vision into a reality.

They also know the pain of not being able to keep up with life after losing a job and fearing how will you maintain everything? Your children are growing up, life now has increasing demands, and you need money for medical checkups. That being said, you need to be guided. Remember, it is not just about the money, it's about the freedom and lifestyle. Forget everything that you have read on the internet about making money and generating passive income streams.

We will reveal some tried and tested methods that have been learned over the course of time. With a lot of research in the field, we bring to you financial strategies focused on the creation of the dream lifestyle.

Did you know that you can actually add an extra income stream to your existing cash flow without increasing your expense and without decreasing your standard of living? Yes, that's actually happening.

Financial planning plays an integral role here. Not only will it help you plug financial leaks or manage taxes, but also build additional streams of income that can support your desired lifestyle. Financial planning is about taking care of your finances in a manner that you can relax at any given point in time. Now you might be wondering what distinguishes us from the sea of financial planning tools in the market. Well, let me address that concern. This book has been synthesized after a lot of research and hard work. Taking into account the lives of the financially successful, it can be inferred that financial planning is a part of their daily regime.

Now, we want you to discover the lifestyle that brilliant marketing and great communication can open up to you. Become an expert communicator and brilliant marketer, and you will truly be able to live the life you see when you close your eyes and dream!

With money being a scarce resource, we want you to put it to the most efficient use. Thus, aim for profit maximization and an increase in efficiency with personal and business finances.

What if you could immediately add extra income to your bottom line? How important is it to recover lost cash flows? Where are your biggest cash flow leaks? If these are your major concerns, you are at the right place.

Discover cash recovery techniques, strategies, and ideas so that you can keep more of what you make. We will help you create cash flow for life. These strategies have proven to help entrepreneurs and small business owners manage their everyday cash flow efficiently.

We want you to retire to a lifestyle you have always imagined; a lifestyle that you see with your eyes closed and always dream of living.

Imagine what your life will look like as you increase cash flow, reduce your tax liabilities, and successfully grow your business. How important is this to you and your family? The decisions you make today will determine the quality of your lifestyle tomorrow.

Don't wait! Take action now. With the right guidance, you can absolutely live the life of your dreams. Anxious to make your life take a U-turn!

What Do You Think About Wealth ?

Are You Ready To Create More Wealth?

We believe anything is possible if WE believe it enough. It's all in our mind, and all you need is to empower it. As a starter, don't let your mind control you. Rather, you should be the one controlling it. This is the only thing that will enable you to jump heaps of uncertainty while winning it every time.

Nothing gives more satisfaction than seeing people reconnect with their soul and treating themselves gently. Our greatest accomplishment lies in witnessing positive changes in people just because they choose to look beyond the horizon. This is what we are here for.

It's that time of life where we want to tell you how satisfying it is to live the life you have always wanted to live. Let us tell you a little secret. When life demands change, we all come up with every possible reason not to change.

Like you, everyone has always resisted change.

Undergoing change would mean:

1. You have a more fulfilling life
2. You would be making more money
3. You will have a sense of purpose
4. You would be financially independent
5. You will have more time to spend on yourself and your loved ones

On the other hand, this is a list of reasons not to change. You might have your own set of ifs and buts.

1. You don't have enough time to learn
2. You are living a stable life
3. You are making enough money
4. You are just not smart enough
5. You can't control your life

The list goes on, and you blame yourself to be even thinking about it while there are so many reasons not to do it. But you know what? You end up thinking more about it.

The reasons as to why you should change your life and why you shouldn't hold equal weightage. However, the reasons calling you to take charge and turn over your life are far more valid, important and rational. Once you are done weighing the risks and rewards, you will land at the fact that the rewards are far greater than the risks. However, human thinking lurks us into fear and we focus on the negative outcomes.

You can only change your life once you break the barriers and take the leap towards positivity. You will say for yourself: life has been so much better since then.

So are you ready? Ready to create more wealth?

The Paths Towards Growth

Did you know that the six best doctors are sunshine, water, rest, air, exercise and diet? Do you have all of these in your life? If you answered no to any of these; you need to get serious. Life happens only once, and you have to make it worthwhile.

The rich live a life they love and help others do the same with the same enthusiasm. They are very passionate about living life on their own terms and live a healthy life inside out. They want everyone to live a life on their own terms. Wouldn't it be great if you are able to do that too?

Here are a few questions we want to ask you!

Are you tired of your life? Are you looking for opportunities to expand your life? Are you looking for financial freedom?

Are you really planning to go on a family vacation but couldn't find the time to do so?

Have you been declining reimbursements?

Are you worried about paying for your child's college fee?

Are you struggling to take care of your health?

We are here to help!.

What do you think will happen if you continue living in your nutshell? Wouldn't life be different if you were able to choose what you've always wanted to do? Wouldn't life be better with smooth finances and a healthy body? It definitely would be. You know that, and you mustn't forget that.

If you are waiting for your knight in shining armor, you ought to stop waiting. You are your savior yourself.

Rich habits help you earn at your terms. All you need to do is to become a mindset and accountability freak with expert knowledge on health and fitness.

Wondering why we are telling you all this? We want you to live a life that's all about spending time with family and having fun.

All the while you make it worthy enough of living, just make sure you don't forget yourself. Take care of yourself because you deserve the best.

This is your opportunity to turn your life around. Make it the best life you've ever had so that you don't have to worry later. You should always feel "this is where I belong."

A few things that you'll learn along the way include:

- Enhancing mindset
- Home business lifestyle
- Prospecting and lead generation
- 6 figure business secrets

You ought to believe in empowerment and prosperity, both of which do not come easy.

Isn't it great that you can actually earn money while taking care of your health? You just need network marketing to do it all, which is a powerful way to earn money in today's world and invest in your future.

Give it a go. Think about it. What if you have a whole network to fall back on? What if you can really escape from the boring life that you're living right now? What if your health is not an overwhelming issue anymore?

It's never been easier to make money while living the life you have always dreamt of.

You need to collaborate with the right people and create a win-win situation for all. That's how it's done. It's done together. The key is to do what you were destined to do, and do it together because ILLNESS becomes WELLNESS when I become WE!

Remember, you need to utilize your potential to fulfill the purpose of your life. Act before it's too late. NOW is the time. NOW is YOUR time.

Although some days will be better than others, you must always look for the blessing. Keep an eye on what life has been trying to tell you. Be positive, stay strong and get enough rest.

You can do it all. You can do your best. You deserve all the happiness in your life, and we are here to help you with that.

The Secret To Your Success Is Hidden In Your Life Story

Like you, everyone has struggled to come up with ideas from time to time. Many of them have not been able to settle for a single thing and know what would enable them to turn their life around. They have wanted to become fiercely independent, sure, but didn't know how they'll achieve the life they want. But you know what has made this so difficult? Do you know what held most of the people from making good amounts of money a few years before? Their COMFORT ZONE! They have been living their lives in a shell and have not really been ready to mingle with anything that would affect their comfort.

Comfort zone made so many people fear the changes they will have to undergo, especially when they were not really ready. But what if you become an independent business owner and run it from your house or a place of your liking? Ever imagined living the life you always dreamt of living, and taking care of yourself and your loved ones. You help people do the same and what can be more rewarding? You play your part in helping others live the life they deserve and suddenly you become a better citizen of this world.

There are two types of people in this world: those that lit up a room when they walked in...And those that lit up a room when they leave. Be the first one. You know why the successful people are successful? They help people with their learning and undertake the journey towards success. But you must know how to access and activate such a lifestyle – then build a WAY OF LIFE that makes it automatic.

That's what people have been doing for years. And that's what we want to help you to do, starting TODAY.

Right now, you need to shake off any doubt, fear, or uncertainty, and take a bold step in the direction of your dreams. Remember, how we do anything is how we do everything. It's so painful to be indecisive. At this point, you know what you need to know, and your inner voice is speaking. The question is, are you ready to listen? Your Destiny is calling.

Millionaires are hard workers. They believe success in life emerges when you are resistant to anything that crosses your path and you simply don't give up. Your success is above every obstacle and all you want is to succeed.

As the clock ticks down, we want to take a moment to check in, see where you're at...Are you looking for opportunities to become successful and earn heaps while creating your own network?

If there's a yes inside, even if it's faint one, covered up by fear, remember the Gospel of Thomas and say YES to your yes. Don't wait for it to 'feel' comfortable, because it NEVER will.

Whatever you're waiting for, you're waiting with – and weighing it down. You must act from your yes to have a breakthrough. That's how real change happens.

If you're thinking things like: 'I don't have enough time right now...I don't have a support system...I don't have the right amount of money... or what if it doesn't work...what if I don't work?!'... Understand that these are all ego threshold responses that are triggered whenever you're feeling an inner yes and are on the brink of real change.

Just look back over your life and notice that you've been here before, maybe many times, and have often backed away from this threshold. That's why you haven't been able to achieve your true potential. That's why the average person keeps on living the same life for all these years.

But if you're feeling the 'yes,' along with some 'buts,' and you are ready to dive, we will together do the work to support that yes and help you anchor yourself at a whole new level.

Have you ever considered the pros and cons of the life you're currently living?

How much time and money will you continue to lose if you don't get clear on your real vision, get committed to living it, and release the unconscious blocks to success? Seriously, what has your lack of clarity, conviction, confidence and consistent action already cost you? In wealth-creation, relationships, creative opportunities?

What has it cost you in happiness and fulfillment? How many more programs or 'strategies' will you try that doesn't address the CORE ISSUES holding you back and sabotaging your success?

You have been there. Spent years trying to fix, change, heal, and improve yourself to success.

So let's work together to make this the best year of your life, so you can look back and say that was truly a happy year and NEW YOU!

We are going to walk you step-by-step through the entire process, so that you will finally:

- Get clarity on your purpose and that too, with absolute confidence.
- Become congruent with success and align your inner self to take action,
- Create a plan of action so that you know what to do, when to do and how to do it, every single day.
- Eliminate procrastination and keep yourself on track, irrespective of what happens.
- Activate your inner wealth mechanism that you are able to generate everything you need.

Trust us, this practice will work wonders. It will help you earn 6 figures and go rich from being broke within a year. However, the main purpose is that you feel good about yourself and the life that you've been blessed with.

A lot of people think that a stable job would suffice their needs. While this is true, it is not enough to help you pursue your dreams. That's what your comfort does to you. So, let's think out of the box. That's what the millionaires do. They develop businesses that help them earn while others make money.

What are you waiting for? Get yourself going and kick start your life. Who wouldn't want a lifetime of investments earning money for them?

Ah, this sounds so good, doesn't it? Let's do this. Together. For the better.

Part 3

Your Chance To Be Your Own Hero

There comes a time when everyone feels frustrated. Everything is messed p! You are disgusted with yourself. Nothing is working out the way you want to. You might have responsibilities to fulfill and it feels so bad to not be able to give your loved ones some of the basics necessities of life. You might have tried to start a business too, that has failed. You're struggling with mental stress. The cherry on top is you have an unfit body. There is too much agony and you think nobody understands. You might be DISGUSTED with yourself. Like everyone, you have the DESIRE to get successful and make money, take charge of your life and become fit.

In this painful moment, make a decision that you will thank yourself for later. It is your moment to do whatever it takes to live the life you have always wanted. You need to feel the valor and determination you are hiding within to turn things around and succeed. You ought to WANT success at any cost. I don't have to be stuck: rather, we have to pave the way.

Now don't think that you will be prepped for all this. No! You won't be! Mark these words: You need to take action when you are not ready. And let us tell you, NOW is the time you take charge of your life. Don't wait for things to be ready. You've got what it takes.

As long as you've got an internet connection, there's no reason you can't be building an empire from your laptop. Remember, the incredible person that you are becoming is going to cost you relationships, spaces, comfort and material things. Choose yourself over everything. You don't want to grow old and regret later. Choose YOURSELF. Look after your health and finances. Trust me; success is the best reward. Treat yourself to all the goodness you deserve. The world awaits you.

The Success Strategy No One Talks About

Lifestyle matters, doesn't it? Did you just answer yes? Just like you, there are many others who are also in search of a lifestyle that's carefree, allows family time and is healthy. Earlier in life, you needed to learn about the importance of starting a business that you don't have to manage actively. There should be something in your life to relieve you from the stresses of finances. The answer to your search leads to finding a business that is based on passive income.

The rich have found the Aladdin's lamp, which has whispered the art of creating 7 figures into their ears.

That being said, the successful and rich are very concerned about their health. They live their everyday life in a manner that doesn't deteriorates their health. We've all known for long how imperative it is to settle early in life and entail a healthy lifestyle, don't we? Who wouldn't brush their teeth before going on a date, or who would go on without bathing for days, just because they are too busy earning the bread and butter? Wouldn't it make a very bad impression?

This might be your pet peeve, and you might have never wanted to come across any of the fellow humans without being in your perfect shape. Here's a success story about a wellness company.

"I was always very concerned about my health and wanted to entail a lifestyle that will help me stay in shape and also earn.

I pondered and pondered, and thereby, I created a company that would make living simple and better. This is how Melaleuca was found. The company went on to become the largest online wellness company in the USA.

Can your logical-self reason with fact as to why Melaleuca gained such a stature? Lifestyle was the answer. Not only there was freedom of time, but also residual income streams. Never had I imagined that a little company I just found as a means of earning will become lifestyle goals for me. I finally succeeded in creating a lifestyle where I could spend more time with my family, and so can you. It's amazing."

This tells that you need to focus on what you really want to do and say no to everything else that isn't that. That's the only way to success.

Your Life's Work Is Hidden Here

Currently many people are worried about the economic climate, concerned about their job and financial security. When you're afraid things could get worse, afraid you could lose money or your job, it could prompt you to accept change when you might otherwise shy away from it and continue down the same dead-end path. To become wealthy you'll need to discard many of your old ways (which probably haven't really worked too well for you up 'til now anyway) and adopt new ideas and strategies. In other words, you have to CHANGE.

You also need to take control of your financial affairs yourself. The problem is many people will find that fear takes over and clouds their judgment when it comes to deciding how to think about money or what to do with their money. Some will even be paralyzed by their fears and choose to remain in the past. If we can change what we believe, we can change what we do. If you keep thinking in this new way, if you keep doing new things, you'll develop new habits. However, if you keep doing what you've always done with regards to money, it's likely that you are going to fall behind and find that you are not left with many choices. You only have to turn on the TV, open the newspaper or browse your iPad to realize you are living in an interesting and, for many, fearful times. Yet there's a lot the average person can do to build and protect his financial security even in the challenging times of today.

We've found that the same events that have made many feel uncertain about their financial future could, on the other hand, produce some of the best opportunities for you to realize your own financial independence. Having said that, there has been a great deal of talk by economists, social analysts, some politicians and the media about our need to lower our expectations and shrink our lifestyles to cope in the current economy. They see the rich getting richer and want them to share more of their money with the rest of the country. This might be a valid advice for those who are prepared to accept governance by circumstance; but lowering our expectations doesn't make sense. As long as there is money, wealth and riches out there it is your right to attract it and acquire it by combining the right thinking, strategies, behaviors and habits that we'll share with you in this book. And there will be opportunities abundantly since we're living in a very exciting financial era — a time of fast change brought about by globalization of many markets and changing technology.

We believe we're living in the best time of history, a time when it's easier to become wealthy than any time before. In the 1900s you needed substantial money to become rich, to become an industrialist or a businessperson. Today, many people have become rich using "intellectual property" or investing in plain old real estate. In fact, more people have become wealthy in the past 20 years than at any other time in human history — which may make you wonder why you haven't become rich. The problem is just because it's easier doesn't mean everyone is doing it. They're not.

A study was conducted for five years, researching the rich and the poor. It was found that only four percent of the poor ever become rich (Kern, 2019). Fortunately, there are a few shortcuts to financial freedom and we're going to share them with you. Having said that, if getting rich was easy everyone would be wealthy. Each year more and more reports are released suggesting very few of us will have enough savings, superannuation or investments to comfortably retire on. And with medical advances meaning that we are all going to live longer, many of us will be forced to work longer in order to fund our retirement. So why do we want you to become rich? There is a saying that we believe to be true: "Any problem that money can solve is not a problem." We've also heard it said that "the state of your wallet plays with the state of your mind". That is, when you have money problems you're likely to also have more stress. Now that's not to say that the rich don't have problems — they do. But the study found that being rich eliminates 67 per cent of life's major problems. That's a pretty big percentage.

Don't Wait To Grow Your Earnings – Automate The Process

Are you one of those people who want to get out of a 9-5 job? If yes, you are at the right place. There are a lot of great things that can happen to you. There are so many people out there who have been living a great life, taking their family on trips and earning 6 figures. However, there might be one issue. You often find yourself on the wishing side rather than doing. This is because you lack clarity.

Here are a few simple truths that will help you down the lane.

1. You are responsible for your happiness. If you are not happy with your life right now, only YOU can change it
2. You ought to bring value to others in order to get paid
3. Money for sure can't buy happiness, but you can buy everything else from it

With these truths, you can focus on a path that helps you reach your goals.

Now you have to decide where do you want to stand? Among people who do the jobs or among business and owners entrepreneurs?

How about knowing a system that operates even when you are not there? The point is; if you stop working, are you going to keep making money? If you are making residual income, you can take months off and still make money. A lot of you don't know how to select a business. You often get bewildered by a lot of flashy things.

Start building your business from your home that expands: a solid sustainable business. The best part? You get to partner with some of the world renowned nutrition, health and lifestyle experts. Did you ever imagine that? We bet you didn't. Start partnering. Start your business.

The Key To The Greatest Success Stories Ever

Before we proceed, we want to steer clear of anything that might hinder the value of what we are offering. We want you to know one thing: anyone can have everything in place for you. They can make the arrangements, tell you how to do it, but they can't do it for you.

The successful ones can give you a roadmap to follow, but some things you learn on your own. You get good at it over time. There's no other way: it's just the hard work that pays off. And while you are along the way of success, their life can serve as a guide, but only when you are committed to move forward. Remember, if you don't take any action, they can't help you. Neither can life coaches do anything for you. While they are pretty awesome at what they do, they can't move something static. You will only succeed because you took the right action. Here's a little story from Diane who paved her way out.

"I work with a friend of mine and help people transition into a successful home based business. That magical person is Steve Swartz, and I'm here because of him. Both of us knew that we wanted more from life. While being grateful is inherently important, I don't imply that you start despising your life. I mean that you entail a clear vision and start moving in the right direction with the prime aim of improving your life. All through these years, I wanted to own my own life, and I struggled a lot to get to this point. I don't want you to go through the same. This could only come through financial freedom and it was then that I decided that I'll work my days and nights to turn my life into the vision I've always had. Don't you want the best income streams that are better than the real estate and stock markets? I'm sure you do."

Then what are you waiting for? Brace yourself for all the goodness that is to come.

Self-Sabotaging Beliefs? Kill tThem And Choose YOU!

Is your life chaotic and stressful and all the negatives you can fit in here? Do you feel overwhelmed and unable to take charge? Don't worry; this book will help you with your inner journey and outer success!

Life is a wonderful opportunity with a ton of potential. You can ALWAYS live the life you want if you take the right actions. Your decisions have a profound impact on how your life turns out to be, and you can make it the most fulfilling one. Are you still thinking that all of what we are talking about seems impossible and it feels like a fantasy?

No it isn't!

Life sure can be stressful and demanding while taking toll on you, but you can always make it better.

Do you know it's possible to launch a profitable business, and that too sitting right back in the favorite corner of your room? All this, for under $500 [that's one option].

No hosting parties and hotel meetings. No stalking. No advertising expenditure. No warehouse!

And the best part? You can do it immediately. Yes, it is totally doable, sitting at your computer at home, making use of a business opportunity.

How? Let us explain.

Let us share a story. Story of Hannibel.

He has come a long way and when he looks back, he finds himself in your shoes. The journey was long and he didn't have anyone to give him all this. You can say he was the guy who was in the rat race, winning it, while still feeling like a rat. He was doing some really cool stuff, but his income was dependent on other people. He didn't want all that. Life was posing challenges and he was faced with too much hassle. That was something he wanted to change. It was then that he stumbled upon a blueprint that helped him make more money, with less stress and less headache. He immediately decided that if it works out for him, he will help everyone that he possibly could. And before he could know it, it was time to fulfill his commitment.

If you are someone who's looking out for ways to change his/her life, you have come to the right place. Here are some important details and tips on how to change your life.

We'll also share some amazing stories that will inspire you to take action immediately. Finally there's someone who cares about you. It's a game changer. It's a lifelong opportunity. Wait no longer. Take action now and start your own business. Be your own boss.

Do You Know Your Life Code?

Do you have questions about health, wellness and finances? Have you heard that the universe continuously responds to you? We are sure you have! Everything you come across, every person you meet, every feeling you feel is there for a reason. The universe is trying to give you signals.

We say that because most of the people ignore these signs for a long time. Although most of them have a thing for the riches and success, they have never thought that it would be something that they would associate themselves with in the long term. And health is a prime concern for success. If you can't take care of yourself, are you even ready for anything else?

The day you experience the loss of a dear one, you will realize how important it is to take care of your body. There are some basic patterns in the lives of the most successful. They are determined to have a healthy life.

Get committed to a healthy lifestyle; rearrange your priorities in life. When you align yourself with the greatest good, you present yourself with numerous opportunities that you can avail with your commitment.

Immediately start your life transformation in the hopes of living the life you have imagined.

The best part is that it's totally possible. Now don't get us wrong, we don't want to sound too persuasive. You can also live a life you see others living. A healthy and financially balanced life.

Financially balanced? YES! We know you've been looking for ways to earn decent money and with too many hoaxes on the internet, you haven't been able to. You are very lucky in this regard. Although it took you time, but you came at the right place. At this point in my life, we can tell you that it all depends on your vision for life. We hope you see your potential and do what you are destined to do.

How To Change Your Entire Life - Create Meaningful Life Experiences

Here's a friendly reminder that life has a lot in store for you, and you are missing out a lot in your life. Have you been looking for a business that will help you earn while enabling you at the same time to serve people around you? Does that sound like you? If this resonates and you consider yourself enthusiastic and passionate enough to transform your life, this is the right place. Never let worries take away your charisma and overburden you with un-needed struggles that will take you nowhere.

When you familiarize yourself with the concept of residual income, you will be beyond amazed. You will be happy that you found something what you had been looking for all your life. Day and night, you will keep thinking about it.

Are you on your way to find a business that will help you make lots and lots of money without waiting forever? Do you want to take control of your life and gear it in the right direction? Don't you want to grant yourself the freedom to live a life you have always wanted and the contentment of serving others?

Let's just say that you can even combine your passions to do this. That's what the rich do. You will often find them combining their passions to build brands. A vivid example is that of independence and wellness.

If you aren't making enough to live the way you want, are you sure you are living right?

We've found the key to success that we want to pass onto you. You just have to trust us. We are telling you the secrets that can't be found on the internet. We want you to be successful. Let's discuss the possibilities for you. The rich build strong relationships with successful people and help you lift up in life. Being the happy and optimistic people that they are, they believe in the power of networking. Developing the tools and systems that can help in networking, remember you can be either rich by association or poor by association. Live upon the fact that you are an average of the five people you spend the most time with.

Moreover, moderation is the key. Successful people live moderately: avoiding addictions, obsessions and extravagances. Every single activity is planned, from the work hours to eating to exercise; their personalities tend to reflect their moderate mindset. A prime example of moderate living is of Warren Buffet, who has been living in the same house since 55 years. He lives simply despite being one of the richest people on the planet. He believes in being the controller of his life, and lives this rich habit every day.

Unsuccessful people, on the other hand, have little control over their lives. They struggle to maintain their lifestyle. They don't have financial safety and savings. An unexpected loss results in financial catastrophe. This highlights the importance of having moderation and prioritizing your needs correctly.

Also, next time someone tells you they are earning six figures, believe them.

The Real Reason You're not Making More

Who doesn't want to have a business while feeling better, staying in shape, having more energy and get better sleep? If you answered yes, carry on.

Have you been dreaming about health and wealth together?

Here's a little breather: your dreams were planted in your heart for a reason. And that reason was not for you to give up on them. Did you know all of this was possible while you make money from it?

Yes, it is possible in case you didn't know. Today is the day to reach out and make it right. Live a healthy and independent life while encouraging others to do the same. Get affiliated with the right people who have been earning and helping others earn as well. Affiliate marketing is one such business that can be literally done in any niche.

Amazing opportunity, isn't it? Tell others and earn a commission as well. We are telling you all this because all the goodness in the world can be shared. We also want you to test it for yourself. You might be hesitant and it's understandable, but trust us, you are missing a whole bunch of independence. Only you can turn things around, and there can be no better time than now. The longer you take to start, the longer it'll be until you get the results. You need to understand this. You need to stop putting your energy into things that lower your vibration. If you are always thinking about financial freedom but stuck at a 9-5 job, you need to be easy on yourself. Give yourself a break. Think things through. Once you are done, start building your empire. There's no excuse for not doing so. All you need to do is; book your meeting. A whole new life awaits you. Build a business soon.

Remember, it's not the business that fails but it is us who fail. Jack Ma, before launching Ali Baba had tried more than twenty businesses which were never successful, but he kept trying. He never gave up. He believed in the idea that businesses don't fail, and he was correct. He now has one of the biggest companies in the world. That's the power of never giving up.

Uncommon Strategies For Sustainable Success

Are you growing weary of life? Ready to take rest because you are not able to put things in sync. Would you like to take control of your life and transform it into the dream life that you always imagined? Well, the good news; it's actually achievable. All you ought to do is leave everything and take action to start your transformation. There's no other way of saying this in fact. You can transform your life the way others around you do. You can live a healthy life, stay put everything else and earn well. You heard it right...earn well!

It is understandable that you want to earn a decent amount of money but don't know how to. Same has been the case with people when they started, but they were soon on the right track. Seizing new and interesting opportunities can help you unravel this secret.

Who wouldn't want a running business that will help them make money while they are not actively taking care of it? It's safe to say that it's all stemmed in how you envision your life... And we can show you do to do it.

If you envision your life as a rich and successful person daily, you will surely get there. Now think about the horse race. Do you know that before the race begins, the horses remain in chaos unless the gun fires and the gates are opened? It is only after the race begins and gates open that the horses are aligned and focused.

Many people are like that. Their race never begins. Their gates remain closed for their lives. That being said, it is important to note that these become habitual thoughts. Unless you get out of the self-sabotaging beliefs, you won't be able to reach the finish line.

The race is the representation of your dreams and goals. And ninety-nine percent of people never get out of the gate because of their thinking. Latest research has proved that the cognitive ability to solve complex scenarios is hindered by negative thinking (Fisher & Allen, 2010). Conversely, positive people have optimistic thoughts that enable them to take the required leap of faith. They are able to create opportunities and devise solutions. They live by the notion that problems and obstacles are nothing but opportunities and learning experiences. Being in control of their thought process, they are able to turn things in their favor.

Discovering the secrets of success, you are sure to work out wonders and find what's waiting for you on the other side of the fence. It's one of the most valuable resources you will ever come across, so don't wait another minute.

The Fastest Way To Heal You - Live A Full And Satisfying Life

Here's just another friendly nudge that life is just around the corner, and we have a strong feeling that you are missing out some serious fun in your life. Never let the obstacles of life make you forget that you can actually make hundreds of dollars while enjoying every little moment with your most precious ones.

Long ago when people got introduced to the idea of residual income, they couldn't resist thinking about it. This story is about the journey Ron undertook to create a business that would make heaps of money, and won't take a lifetime to realize the dream. He never forgot what he wanted to achieve.

Turning your vision in a reality is the best way to live for it allows passion to take control of everything. And nothing can be better than anything done with passion. If you aren't making enough to grant you the freedom to live your life on your terms, are you even actually living? He found the key ingredient to live life on his own terms and generated 89 thousand in commissions in the first year.

If Ron Urban can do it, you can do it too. This will give you the freedom to do whatever you want. Travel, explore, live! We want to tell you the secret. It isn't difficult at all. Rather, it's such a great thing to have that it will make you merry-go-round! You have to take our word for it. This meeting will be a life changer. Although the internet is flooded with information, you can't find the valuable information that I have been longing to tell you.

They say, don't ignore the signs. Everything you are attracted towards is for a reason. Don't you feel that's true? If you have a thing for success and richness; may be that is because you are going to be linked to it forever? But there stands a strong connection with success.

Here's how Ron did it.

"I was committed to raising my son really well, the primary reason being that we lost two children before owing to a kidney disease... And we didn't want to lose him at any cost.

Finally, I was living with a healthy son. This made to committed to a lifestyle that focused on health.

I was working with a company that had an exclusive range of products with no chemicals in them. The best part about that was…

We can be using some amazing products to live healthily while making money out of it. I was instantly hit with an idea. Why don't I tell my friends and family about the super cool products so they can live a healthy life too? Well, I won't hide. Telling them about these products would mean commissions for me. But I NEVER tell anyone about anything that doesn't work! So yeah, the products I planned on telling to others worked wonders! You cannot imagine my excitement. Actually, it was double the joy...

Of course being able to provide my son with the safest wellness products, and being able to generate income from them. Woah! What a deadly combo it was. Life hadn't been this good, and I and my wife were awestruck. I then later discovered about this whole system, and that it's called network marketing. I want you to learn about it too. Let me tell you, I only want to train a few people who take their life very seriously."

If you think you are ready to get your hands on this opportunity, do it now. That's how passive income works.

Feel Inspired And Creative

They say, people don't remember everything about you, but they surely remember how you made them feel. Make this your mission and work hard to make a difference in this world. This world needs a lot of compassionate and kind people. Doing your business can be very basic, for you will be kind and caring towards the people whom you owe the most: your family. Keep that in mind and grow yourself beyond any limitations.

Remember, owning a business is the best thing that you can do to yourself. And as you learn about the key facets of business, know that networking is of prime importance. Although you might not be good at it, you can learn everything about it and seize the opportunity to grow. While none of us is perfect, we must work daily for improving ourselves.

Read this story. Does it sound like you?

"I'm kind, compassionate and caring, but that doesn't stop me from having a fun-filled life. I'm driven by the urge to make this world a better place to live.

I love dogs and cats; I love to help others and I love to travel. All this has been possible because I live a fulfilled, independent life.

But it wasn't like this from day one. I was young and determined when I decided that I will live a life I have always dreamt of. I was unstoppable – but things weren't so clear. Thus I decided to unveil the secret of success for myself. I followed the self-proclaimed networking gurus on the internet and trust me; most of them were nothing but a waste of time. Anyways, I decided to pursue my journey and searched for opportunities that will bring the much needed financial freedom for me. I started to study the rich. I learned sooner that I wanted to be a business builder. I realized that this field had much potential and would be the best fit for a person like me. Long story short, I decided to give it a go and worked days and nights, and here I am.

It was one fine morning when I woke up and I was surprised to see six figures in added revenue. I shouted with excitement: "What? Six figures in added revenue! Woohoo! What a great day."

And that's when it all started. Now if you want to turn your life around, this book is your answer.

This book has the tools and techniques that will help you rearrange your life and live it to the fullest. These tools will provide you with the much needed insight and help address anything that's holding you back. Moreover, these tools will provide you with the right shift and push you out of your comfort zone. Trust us; this will bring you abundance and success. According to modern brain science, there is one force that shapes your career and financial success more than anything else.

Hint: It's not the number of hours you work every week. It's not how self-motivated you are. And it's not even the books you read or the seminars you've attended. It's your direction and we believe with the right direction, you can do anything.

When we say "direction", most of the people think that we are only going to talk about branding and everything general that's available on the internet. Truth be told, when the rich interact with their clients, they talk beyond the 'think and act' philosophy, because while thoughts and actions are important, the secret that actually makes it work is the rightly steered actions. That's when you start manifesting your truest potential.

Imagine a business where you can work from the comfort of your own home and building a residual income that can be passed from generation to generation. You need to interact with some of the most interactive and creative people pursuing their dreams. You help people build their dreams and they help you build yours – and that's how everyone helps each other earn. If you are interested in transforming your life, please start from today. That means you will achieve success faster and easier than ever before.

And because now you know how important it is to live independently, fulfilled life, you can completely trust our secrets. These will take you out of the blues, we promise. On a lighter note, we believe in taking a walk on the Wild Side! With Zebra striping! That means living on the edge.

This Will Double, Triple And Quadruple Your Growth

So, here is why the rich are actually rich.

They invest their money wisely, watch over their investments regularly and set realistic goals for their investment returns. They have high credit scores, know their net worth and monitor their personal balance sheet. They use only the most qualified financial professionals to maximize their returns and minimize their taxes. They employ the services of experts like certified public accountants, certified financial planners or attorneys. They use these professionals to help them manage their money and their taxes.

They participate to the fullest extent permitted by law in retirement plans. Many of these retirement plans allow individuals to put away, in a tax-deferred manner, a large portion of their income each year. If their company does not have a retirement plan, they create their own retirement plan by funding individual retirement accounts. They add to these accounts with every pay cheque. They have retirement goals. They monitor their retirement plan regularly and make course corrections in an effort to reach their retirement goal.

They live pay day to pay day, spending every penny to support their lifestyle. They are poor savers and carry excessive amounts of debt. They have home equity loans, which are tapped out. Their credit cards are maxed out, and they can barely make the monthly minimum payments. They have poor credit scores. Unsuccessful people don't contribute to retirement plans. Some gamble excessively and view the lottery as their retirement plan. They take risks, which are either unnecessary or not well thought out. They don't set aside at least 10 per cent of their income and, consequently, when they reach the age of retirement, they don't have enough retirement savings to allow them to retire with financial security. They rationalize that they can't afford to set aside 10 per cent of their earnings. They are unwilling to alter their lifestyle in order to save adequately. More often than not, unsuccessful people have no choice but to continue working well into their retirement years or rely on family or the government.

Successful people are the masters of their words and emotions. They understand that saying whatever is on your mind could damage relationships with individuals who could help move them forward in achieving their dreams. They don't fall prey to anger, jealousy, excitability, sadness or other petty emotions. They cast out all bad emotions. They don't allow them even a second of their life. They understand that negative emotions cause them to make bad decisions that result in bad consequences. They replace these bad emotions with positive emotions.

When facing a critical situation, they think, evaluate and react. Thinking gives them time to understand the situation. Evaluating the situation buys more time to determine the correct course of action. Reacting is the last thing they do and most likely will be the appropriate reaction, as they took the time to choose their reaction. Our everyday words create perceptions for us. Acting as magnets, they draw you to different types of realities. The rich knew this way before they became rich. These words create realities.

Successful people are much aware of the words they use when they communicate to others. They choose words that won't offend others. They use words to reinforce the perception they have of themselves and use their words to also rein- force the perception others have about them. Successful people are too busy to allow themselves to sink into a negative emotional state. They engage in productive activities, which take their minds off their troubles. They are constantly engaged in projects or self-improvement activities that promote positive feelings about themselves. Successful people feel as if they have total control over their emotions. Unsuccessful people are unaware of the words they are using every day. They unknowingly use words that offend others, damaging relationships. They use words that create a perception in the eyes of others that is not favorable. Unsuccessful people fall prey to petty emotions. They let their emotions rule their behavior. They become easily depressed and feel as if they have no control over their lives. They react before thinking. They have adopted the bad habit of "Ready, Fire, Aim." As a consequence of this, there are many unsuccessful people sitting in prisons throughout the world.

Part 4

Did You Get On The Ladder To Success

How do you take your ladder off someone else's wall and move it to your own wall? Successful people pursue work that they love. Because they are doing work that they love, they devote more time to it. They get labeled as "workaholics", which is ironic because they never actually feel like they are working hard at all. To them work is play. It's fun and it's enjoyable. They look forward to it. Because they are devoting more time to their work, they become expert in what they do. The ones who become successful find what they really love and how it can be monetized, which fills them with passion. Success takes time. Those who succeed never quit. Long-term persistence is a requirement for success.

There is a universal step of climbing the ladder of success. Believe in yourself, take action and don't accept any excuse that holds you back, and always stay focused; look for strategies to seek help in your projects, in case of hardships, do not be scared of making mistakes along the way and don't be afraid of taking unusual decisions. Be courageous, be ambitious and when you see the signs of success, do not let yourself to be carried away by avarice, keep yourself in the midst of positive people and keep a cool head. That will assist you in progressing with your personal development and the development of your project.

Avoid the negative people, work harder, don't get distracted by the trolls and don't let anyone come in between you and your success. The question that arises is: why are some people miserable while others are happy on their journey? What exactly is that factor that motivates people to reach a higher level of success and what are the things they put into practice that help them improve? Burchard, the world's leading high performance coach carried out an extensive research, at the end of the research, he discovered that it is only six deliberate habits that gives you an edge, he said, that anyone can carry out these habits deliberately and, when they do, they start to achieve extraordinary things, they achieve greater things in their lives, careers and relationships (Burton, 2012). These habits can assist you in achieving long term success no matter your sex, age, personality, career or strength. To operate in a high level of success and enjoy a lasting success at the peak, there are certain things that must be done. You must seek clarity, develop influence, demonstrate courage, generate energy, raise necessity, and increase your level of productivity. In this book, you will learn about the art and science of how to practice and cultivate these proven habits. Whether you want to improve certain part of your skills, be a good leader, want to increase productivity, or increase drastically your sense of joy and confidence, the habits discussed in this book can assist you greatly and help you achieve it faster. Each of the six enlisted habits are practically explained with powerful thought provoking exercises, a cutting-edge science and real-world technique that you can implement.

Search for clarity

More often than not, people with a very high performance don't wait till the eve of the new year before having a self-assessment and having to think about the type of change they want in their lives, rather, they seek clarity on a day to day basis, they are create a self-awareness of the changes in their lives. A simple way to deploy this, is to have more focus on these four things; skills, self-confidence, social and human service. Let's take for instance, how can you describe your ideal self? How do you want to interact socially? What are the skills you want to develop or improve? What are the services that you wish to render? These are the questions you should be frequently asking yourself. Generating energy Lots of people tend to lose energy while making a transit between different tasks, responsibilities or meetings. Meanwhile, people of extraordinary performance, when faced with such transition, try to dominate, they take some psychological break that releases them of some tension, doing this, they get relieved and renewed their approaches in facing each task. Every day they find time to relax, and this boost their level of creativity.

Raise the need

It's important for you to know the psychological need to be functional before you engage in a task. High performance people tend to have a deep sense of excellence and perform at their highest standards; this is associated with their identity. They have a passion to do things right, they dedicate their activity towards achieving the best possible result for their clients, teammates, or family. They always tend to do things perfectly.

Increase in productivity

This is a trait that is common to all high-performance geniuses like Bill Gates, Steve Jobs, Arianna Huffington and Oprah Winfrey (Ali, 2016). They know the importance of the end result. To be a productive person, you need to always be steps ahead and align yourself to achieve your goals while learning to manage anything that could cause distractions and avoid other forms of distractions. Building a positive influence on others Affecting people's lives, teaching them to reason, challenging them to grow and improve is essential. Also, having a positive impact on their lives, pushing them to their limit, awakening their flexibility and sensitivity is also crucial.

Because, all those who are capable of making positive impact have a way of contributing towards the growth of others.

Demonstrate value

In the face of risk, fear of the unknown and difficulty, high performance people stand tall; they speak for themselves, keep their focus, and honor the struggle by adapting and learning to manage the situation. We can say that they "embrace" the difficult moments, instead of wailing and complaining or giving up, they identify their mission, keep their head cool, use it as a learning curve and sail the tide. They embrace the situation with purpose and make meaning out of it.

Find Your Team – It's Imperative

Did you know; Steve Jobs had Steve Wozniak?

Bill Gates had Paul Allen.

Warren Buffet had Charlie Munger.

It remains an incontestable reality that self-made millionaires are always supported by their circle and that's how they get there. The wealth that they accumulate is persuaded through pursuit of a dream. And most of the times, it is a team effort. People who have elevated themselves to the status of a millionaire tend to be the ones who have found their apostles – passionate individuals who share their dream. Probably the most famous individual who found the yang to their yin was Jesus Christ. He actually found 12 apostles to help him spread his important message and his cause. Jesus succeeded, not simply because of the importance of his message, but because he found 12 others who also believed in his message and his cause. If it were not for his apostles, the world would not know about Jesus or his message. Successful people are able to put together a team of one or more individuals who buy into their dream and their goals. They are able to find individuals who commit themselves 100 per cent to their cause. Successful people understand that finding apostles to their cause turns dreams into reality. Unsuccessful people are not very good at building teams to help them succeed in life. They do it alone and hope for success. But finding apostles is never easy. Many times, people attracted to you and your dream will not become your associates. It is extremely difficult to find people who will share your vision with you. People you often come across tend to pursue their own projects and dreams. What you ought to do is to continue your search unless you find the right people. Only one right person and the magic will happen. Anyone who has struggled in finding their yang knows it's a very difficult and frustrating journey. The right apostles are those who commit to your dream. They become fanatics to your cause. Their commitment is 100 per cent. Finding your "apostles" means you've found a team who will all pull the same cart? Apostles will have a single- minded focus; they will all be devoted to turning your dream into a reality.

You need to get the best team you can around you — if you are the smartest person in your team, you are in trouble. You need to surround yourself with a team of professionals including a tax-savvy accountant, a smart lawyer who can help you with asset protection, a proficient mortgage broker and an independent property investment strategist — not one who sells property or has a vested interest in helping the vendor or project developer, but someone who is independent and truly on your side. At first you might be reluctant to pay for advice, because there seems to be so much "free" advice available in books, on the Internet, in chat forums, etc. Here's the best piece of free advice you will receive — free advice is very expensive . We've heard someone call the cost of the mistakes most investors make trying to do it on their own a "stupid tax". You won't ever get to Level 3 or 4 on the Wealth Pyramid and develop financial independence without a team of professionals who share your vision, appreciate your efforts and understand the principles of wealth creation.

Find Yourself A Mentor

Mentors can help you to become rich by contributing to your wealth creation in the following ways:
- Imparting knowledge: a mentor can bring a wider range of experience to the table and offer you the opportunity to gain years of knowledge in a short time span. This could be a personal mentor or you could

learn from someone who has done it before through a book, a DVD or seminar.
- Sharing experience: we are all taught to learn by trial and error, but you should learn from somebody else's mistakes, rather than make costly errors yourself. A good mentor will have a thorough understanding of the dos and don'ts to help prevent you making your own mistakes.
- Mentors make you present your ideas and then make you think long and hard about your ideas and what you're planning to do justifies what you are planning to do.
- Providing contacts: a good mentor will have contacts that can help you seek out and identify opportunities you wouldn't have found yourself. Having a wide range of contacts will help you enormously.
- Mentors can motivate you and help you achieve in different areas that you
Might not have thought you could find success in.
- Mentors can save you time: having done it before, they can show you the shortcuts and teach you the potholes to avoid, helping you to navigate and take the right turns on your road to riches.
- Mentors are independent and won't have a vested interest in what you do, so they can offer you support. They'll understand when you're feeling high and why you're feeling low at times and they can relate to the challenges you will go through on your climb up the ladder to being rich and successful.

A Few Critical, Often Overlooked, Steps To Lasting Success

One of the key to success for those who climb the Wealth Pyramid is surrounding themselves with supportive people and recognizing the right friends and network of people who can provide support and encouragement along the way. You see... our peers, the people we associate with, have a great deal of influence over us because they make up our group affiliations.

As humans we are innately social beings; we like to form groups for comfort, support and security. Over time these groups develop their own set of values and morals, which become our reference model for how we interact with the wider world. These groups can consist of our families, friends, churches, clubs, golfing partners or whatever. Many of us crave these informal group associations because they give us a sense of identity and companionship as we move through life. We like to belong to groups and if you think about it, since our group affiliations have such a profound impact on our personal values and priorities, it's important that we associate with supportive and optimistic people as we strive for a better life.

Unfortunately, our world is filled with pessimistic people who often keep us from moving forward and finding the success and joys that we desire in life. One of the tragic mistakes we've seen too many people make on their road to success is listening to all the critics along the way. Too many people put a lot of emphasis on the silly advice of unsuccessful people. This is particularly evident when people are feeling nervous after hearing or reading all the negative messages the media keeps feeding them. So why is it that some people tend to be very unsupportive? Obviously there's not one clear answer, but let's explore this for a moment. Some people are naturally unsupportive because they have not been able to find happiness in their own lives. It boils down to this: for many, another's success merely highlights their personal failures. Of course, this even happens with family or friends. Another reason people are unsupportive is because they are jealous or envious. Envy is just an advanced degree of the old green-eyed envy monster, but what we really mean is when some people wish that they had what their friends already possess — they covet their friends' success rather than celebrate it. And since the envious person doesn't have what his friend already has, they wish their friend didn't have it either.

Millionaire Success Practice - How To Overcome Any Obstacle

Do you ever wonder why can't you make enough money, just like those influencers claim? The answer is actually very simple: you're looking in the wrong direction. They are no different than you. They just know WHEN and HOW to take the RIGHT action in the RIGHT direction. You can be one of them, too... And you want to be one of them, but you don't how what to do...so you start making an effort...however, that's uninformed and does no good.

Now, we are cent percent sure that you are not doing that on purpose... Why would one intentionally do something that is of no good? But sometimes, it is looking in the wrong direction that represents a quest for attaining something in life... something that can help us do better, perform better, earn better, live better. That quest can be fueled by anything...from taking care of a family to the worry of making ends meet. Whatever that might be; the wrong direction has crossed your path for a reason... When you to realize the right direction and it enables you to set your life straight.

But the thing is; it's not that simple. You need to put in some effort in order to know the secrets of earning well. But the good news is; I can reduce half of the efforts, so you never go astray. If you are ready for the transformation, we will show you how it's done!

Living the rich habits is the answer. You need to be vigilant of yourself and practice gratitude. You need to stay away from the negative mindset and practice success. Here are the traits of negative minded people that you need to avoid at all costs:

- Victim mindset
- Closed mindedness
- Ideological constraints
- Intellectual constraints
- Immediate gratification

On the contrary, positive affirmations can help you reprogram your brain towards success and turn it into a powerful tool. Directing behavior, your brain will then use these positive affirmations, channeling you towards success.

Here is a list of positive affirmations that you should practice every day.

- I accomplish my goals
- I complete whatever is on my list daily

- I am successful
- I am worthy
- I make $400,000 a year
- I am running a successful company
- I love what I do
- I have a great lifestyle
- I am the controller of my life

These affirmations give a signal to your brain about the reality you want to create for yourself. Note that they have to be specific and in the present tense. Make your own list and practice them daily. Have a grasp on it and unlock your truth. Isn't it simple? Yes, it is. Let your worries fade away.

Create Your To Do List – Everything Else Goes On Not To Do List

Successful people are much aware of the things they should not be doing as they are of the things they should be doing.

People have made more money in their life by saying "no" to things than by saying yes to perceived opportunities. But not only do we have a to-don't list regarding business and investment, we have a very long one for your life which includes the following:

- Don't worry — most of the things you worry about will never occur and those that will are likely to seem petty in five years' time.
- Don't always be right — I've found that often in relationships you can be right or be happy — so be selective in your battles. There are many roads to the right destination.
- Don't look at things from a short-term perspective — take a wider view.
- Don't follow the crowd — don't do what everyone else is doing, because if you do, at best you'll be average.
- Don't wait for the perfect time — there will never really be a "right time" for anything in life.
- Don't wait to start until you know everything — that time will never come.

- Get started, knowing you don't have all the information, and learn and improve along the way.
- Don't judge other people — it's easy to jump to conclusions — but that's prejudgment or bias. Instead listen and try to understand the other persons' point of view.
- Don't try to be perfect — sure you should strive for the best, but let go of perfectionism.
- Don't brood over your mistakes — they're part of growing and learning so don't think of what could have been done.
- Don't ignore your friends and loved ones — after all, your true wealth is what you're left with when they take all your money, property and stocks away.
- Don't neglect your present joys — this is the Rich Habit of being grateful.

Make A Living Doing What You Love – And Inspire Others

Who doesn't know the power of a smile?

We are sure you do! It gives a powerful signal, a signal of encouraging people, of lending kindness and showing love, and we love to encourage other people. We also know how soothing it is to travel and work from a place of your liking?

Imagine how you'd feel to create your own flexible schedule with the freedom to choose the work and wake up every morning with the excitement to work. Wouldn't you feel great to have an extra income that supports your family and lets you have crazy travel adventures? This is the type business that will allow you to work at ease, from anywhere, at any time you want. Now don't worry about having a business plan that you've been searching for all these years! We know you've wanted to be in business ever since and you've searched for the right business plans, but destiny had something else in store for you.

If it has brought you here, it might be a signal for you. May be, you are destined to become a millionaire, and once you are on your way, trust us; you wouldn't want to be in anything else. Helping you with a life that's built in your favor is what gets us excited. That is what gets us closer to accomplishing our mission of helping everyone listen to their true calling.

We believe in the beauty of dreams, and the fact that they do come true. Only when you see how beautiful this life is, can you sing along, dancing on the tune life sets for you? Okay, back to basics. We all are young at heart and thus we don't let anything get in our way to success. We are telling you now: go after what you want. And that's what you should do!

The main reason why the rich continue to grow rich is the sense of self-accomplishment. And trust us; no other feeling comes close to it.

It allows them to maximize their efficiency and effectiveness. They apprehend that they are destined to achieve, and deliver what they were created for, without wasting any energy. Your energy is precious too. Before the time goes out, you should control your life and turn it in your favor. Use your potential before it uses you! If you are serious about creating a solid income stream with all the independence and freedom that you desire, this is your ideal stop.

Remember, successful people are risk takers. They take risks that make other cower in fear. Risk is a necessary component of success. You cannot possibly succeed without taking risk. But the risk we are referring to is not the type of risk that gamblers take. The risk successful people take is known as calculated risk. This is a type of risk that requires thoughtful analysis. It requires that you study all the variables of any initiative that involves some risk. Calculated Risk means you've identified every potential scenario that could lead to failure. When you take Calculated Risk, you prepare yourself for all possible contingencies. It requires a lot of work and thought. As a result, you are never blindsided when something goes wrong. You never panic when things go wrong. You have a well thought-out contingency plans for every problem that comes your way. You're prepared for the worst. That's calculated risk.

Fall Down 7. Get Up 8

Are you someone who is always in search of ways of stepping up your life? You are always on the lookout for something that will prove to be a game changer for you? But alas! You do not succeed in doing so. Don't you want something that will help you move forward in your life and unleash your truest potential? Don't you want a life where you are in control? Don't you want to be only one in charge of your life's affairs? We know you do, and that's why we are here. We'll help you unlock the mysteries of your life.

We believe in getting a new perspective so as to be able to see life in limelight. Get to know this, and learn how to unleash your true potential.

The secret lies in millionaire secrets. The goal is to enrich the lives of everyone around it. Whether you are an independent marketing director or a part of the corporate staff, these secrets provide you with opportunities to grow. The aim is to have everyday savings. It believes in unleashing the entrepreneurial spirit while encouraging honor, integrity and character in all aspects of life and business.

The aim is simple: to take you from where you are to a much better, happier, more fulfilling life and to make you financially independent, have savings and enjoy your life. Gaining financial independence will help you steer your life in the right direction. This way, you'll learn to navigate your powers and will be fully prepared to take advantage of anything that comes your way.

You know these seemingly rich and successful individuals go through a lot of annoyance when they decide to take charge of their life and make the positive changes in their life. The changes that they try to make are scaring to the, they are unable to decide for good. Success is anything but easy. For the longest time, you might be unable to decide whether you will be able to do it and whether the decision towards financial independence will make you land towards success.

While you knew deep down that this is the life you always desired, yet you are so afraid to jump out of your comfort zone that you have created for yourself. However, everything is much impactful and you ought to decide that you will do it no matter what it takes. That is when you will be able to do it with a lot success. The rich who-seem-to-have-it-all does it this way.

That being said, you can do it too. Now, you might be inquisitive about how will you? We know it's doable because people all over the world have done it. Anyone can. And we are here to support you throughout your journey.

You need to stop waiting for someone to come save you. You're your own savior. You need to stop doubting because you've got it all. You need to start investing in yourself and that's the best thing you can do to yourself. Waste no more time. Do it today.

The What If Game

While unsuccessful people give in to the voices, successful people ignore those voices. They pursue goals, dreams, new business opportunities and new challenges in life in spite of the fears and the doubts that they have. How is it that successful people are able to overcome the negative voices of doubt and fear? Successful individuals play something I call The What If Game:

- What if I succeed?
- What if I love doing this?
- What if I make more money than I expect?
- What if it's not as hard as I thought?
- What if it makes me happy?
- What if it helps my family?
- What if it creates the life of my dreams?
- What if it makes me more valuable?

Playing the What If game will help you steer clear of all negativity that surrounds you and replace it with goodness and positivity. All your fears and doubts will fade away and you'll experience a refreshed mindset. You will get the courage to move forward. Remember, next time whenever you face a difficult decision, play the What If game.

Make A Living Doing What You Love

You must become the role model for your children, so when they grow up, they know what they ought to do. Develop a mindset that focuses on abundance and growth (Burnette et al., 2019). Why? Because growth and abundance are your greatest assets.

Every person has great skills and when guided, everyone can earn themselves recognition, and mothers are great at it. We want to make successful entrepreneurs out of our parents so they can live a life they love while building a successful stay-at-home business.

Wondering why do we say that? Well, parents have a ton of skills they use regularly. They are multi-tasking, creative, entail problem-solving capabilities and know how to operate on a budget. Isn't it just amazing that all these skills combined can help you run a wonderful business? You need to put all your energy in the right place for the universe to respond to you. Whatever you do, you can help your children achieve more in their lives.

But don't you dare think all this will come easily. They say "hustle till you bustle". The rich have rich life because they have been putting in the work when everyone else was busy feeling too tired. You should be the type of person who always reminds others to dream bigger and better. You should have goals so big that you get uncomfortable talking to people about them. You have to do it!

You need to think like an entrepreneur to become one (now you see where we are coming from). Everything begins in your mind, and if you get your mindset right, you can achieve anything you imagine.

Wondering why we are telling you all this? Probably because we know how overwhelming life can be and because everyone is challenged one way or the other, we want you to be your own savior and be in control of your destiny. Rediscover your self-worth and develop a burning desire to make anything possible. You are stronger than you think. Is it easy? No! It takes commitment, hard work and a little more self-recognition. But, when you're building a dream life, something that you can truly be proud of, it's sure is worth everything. You need to focus on your future self and tell if it'd be proud of what you are doing today. If you answered yes, NOW is the time. BRING IT ON!

Stop doubting yourself and stop procrastinating. You need to have an action plan to live a happy and healthy life. You need to fit in your plan and do everything that it takes to make yourself better, healthier and happier.

30 Ways That Makes The Rich Different

So now, we are telling you 30 Rich Habits that can change your life with a little effort and commitment to change. Here they are to help you make them part of your life — right now!

1. The rich and successful adopt good daily habits and follow them religiously every single day.
2. Defining the dreams and creating goals around them, they focus on dream goals daily.
3. Devoting a set time period every day to increasing their knowledge and skills, they invest in themselves for their future.
4. At least 30 minutes of every day is devoted to exercise. They eat healthy food every day as a self-care measure.
5. They seek to build strong relationships with other success-minded people.
6. They live moderately and closely monitor it.
7. They are devoted to take step steps towards their goals every single day.
8. They think rich and act rich – it is important to think and act rich every day and live like you are already rich.
9. They save a specific amount of their income and spend the rest. You can decide your saving to be ten to twenty percent, spending any amount that remains.
10. They control their words and emotions every day.
11. They do work that they love and are passionate about.
12. They never quit on my dreams.
13. They embrace only positive beliefs and eliminate all negative beliefs.
14. They seek out success mentors.
15. They focus on their dreams and goals every day.
16. They set only good goals and avoid bad goals.

17. They do not fear risk. They take risks that help them achieve their goals and realize their dreams.
18. They exercise patience every day.
19. They seek to exceed the expectations of others.
20. They create multiple streams of income.
21. They use the power of leverage to help them achieve their goals and realize their dreams.
22. They do not allow fear or doubt to prevent them from taking action on their goals and dreams.
23. They seek feedback from others.
24. They ask for what they want or what they need.
25. They make their own personalized to-don't list and follow it every day.
26. They ask questions in order to learn from others.
27. They seek to give to those deserving of their time without any expectation of benefiting.
28. They make an effort to be happy every day.
29. They train others how to treat them.
30. They seek to find apostles to help them achieve their goals and realize their dreams.

Learnt The Success Habits? Apply Them Next – That's The Only Way Forward

Don't you often think how people become millionaires? Do you wonder that they find the magic lamp that turns the things around for them? No. They are the Genie themselves! They take charge of their life and do what they always wanted to do. Like you, they are the ones stuck in their life but are desperate to become financially independent. They want to be accountable to no one but themselves.

There are so many people who earn millions just through seizing the right opportunity. Do you realize that there is an earning opportunity in it for you too? You can earn massively and help others live a better life as well. What else one could ask for. Do you buy in the idea of helping your fellow beings live healthily while you build your business? You can have two visions combined: serving others and building your own business. Now, you need to get started too. They say, together you go farthest.

Do you want change and growth? Do you want to be on a mission to empower people live their purpose? Do you want to be part of a purpose that helps create a world that works for the highest good of all?

If so, learn new business practices. Learn and share. That's a vivid trait of all the successful people. Do not waste your precious time and keep wandering in quest of something genuine. Develop the possibilities of achieving your business goals and act immediately. Visualize your future and think of how you can provide valuable solutions to those around you? This will bring you the most success. Use your personal strengths in your business and become a brand. Become a strategic planner so the return on equity can be increased. Enhance the financial results and develop better business habits.

The opportunity has knocked at your door. Seize it now rather than have regrets later. Become a winner. Develop the determination to win, outperform your competition and ultimately triumph.

Become Part Of A Mastermind Group

Another habit for business success is the habit of masterminding with other people, both inside your company and outside. The result is absolutely astonishing! Very often, entrepreneurs who have been struggling with business questions and problems for many months get solutions from the members of their mastermind group in a matter of minutes. A mastermind group can be either structured or unstructured. Either one will be effective. In a structured mastermind group, a particular question such as, "How can we increase sales in this market?" is thrown out and everyone brainstorms different ideas that they have found or are trying in their own businesses. Very often, an idea that has proven successful in one type of business is exactly the idea that works successfully for a completely different business. In an unstructured brainstorming session, people get together and "free-flow." They talk in general terms about business, the economy, sales, customers, competitors, and so on. Out of this ferment often come great ideas that members of the mastermind group can use in their own activities. If you own your own business, you should sit down with your key people and mastermind a couple of times each week. Talk about how the business is going and some of the problems that you are facing. Ask if anyone has any suggestions or ideas. Listen attentively without interrupting when people make suggestions. Go around the table and invite input from everyone. You will be absolutely amazed at the quality of ideas that seem to emerge when you practice masterminding and brainstorming on a regular basis.

Unveiling this secret to you, this happens to be one of the most powerful tools that successful people use — whether they were rich industrialists in the early 20th century or today's super achievers — is that they were part of a Mastermind Group. Napoleon Hill discovered the power of a Mastermind Group and wrote about it in his acclaimed book — *Think and Grow Rich* — almost 100 years ago. Just to make it clear, this is an alliance of two or more people who work together for the achievement of a definite purpose in a spirit of mutual harmony and cooperation. When you form a Mastermind Group, we're not talking about positive thinking or affirmations; it's another easy way of reprogramming yourself for success. While it is imperative that you work hard to become successful, a Mastermind Group can help you harness your focus.

Rich Habits – Busting The Myths

Do you know the urge to live a wealthy and independent life that makes people stumble upon success?

They invest their money wisely, watch over their investments regularly and set realistic goals for their investment returns. It is one such wise decision that they are on a lookout for companies that enable them to network and earn. Wouldn't you like to be associated with one such company?

The best part is that being affiliated with such companies will enable you to earn. Are you perplexed? Why didn't such an opportunity cross you before? Well, there's time for everything.

The rich and successful see an unimaginable opportunity in everything: they are on a lookout. They start to make money, and they instantly feel the urge to tell others around them to do the same. They are firm believers that any joy shared is double the joy...and they want to double their joy of earnings. Isn't it so cool? We want you to try this out. We know you don't like to try new things, but trust us; you are missing a whole lot of things. Only you can make your life better, and NOW is the time to act. We hope to see you build a business soon.

And Some Success Stories

Do you desire a way to live your deeper purpose in a way that allows you to make a living doing what you love? Maybe you're a coach, healer, or spiritual entrepreneur who gets overwhelmed by heavy energies -- and you need more support to give full expression to what's in you...

Perhaps you find the idea of building a business and being in the world in a bigger way too daunting and stressful to go for it in a consistent way...

The great news is that you can use meditation as a master key to align with your greatest purpose and gifts -- in a way that allows you to make an impact AND income with more ease.

It's the same approach that Oprah, Eckhart Tolle, Neale Donald Walsh, and many other spiritually-inclined teachers and healers have done it.

You are probably thinking what I do to get such a good life? Just like you, there was a time when the now successful were looking up to someone who would hold their hand and guide them through everything. Now here's another success story.

"I was always looking for opportunities throughout my life that will enable me to establish a business and build an empire. Finding my dream job became my ultimate objective in life and I started to struggle. While I did not know the right direction, I was just hustling, hoping it would take me places. As time passed, I got to know what would be beneficial for me, and I thereby entered the world of entrepreneurship. I began to love my life, and what once seemed like an unattainable plan was now actually happening. It then dawned upon me that this was what I have been looking for my entire life. I was finally living my dream.

The life-changing event that took place helped me gain perspective. I got involved in the idea of creating my own business…nothing else would attract me…I was constantly working on ways to explore my idea. Basically, what scared me the most was the fact that someone else is controlling me as the boss…I didn't want that. So, I was trying to make things work that would make me my own boss.

That was when I came across a company that would enable me to make money while helping me earn massively. I totally bought in the idea. Now that I have found what I was looking for, I want others to learn about it too.

The reality is, I didn't have any help when I needed it. But I don't want you to feel that way too. I want to help you out so you can live a better life. I believe it's done best when done all together. That said, are you ready for it? Will you allow me to help you?

I really hope you do, because who wouldn't want to be prosperous? I also want you to know that you have got it what it takes. Please take your chance, take the risk. I am sure you don't want to miss out this great opportunity. If I were in your place, I would have never let it go."

And another one:

"I was searching for options and trying to discover what can help me achieve the life I've always wanted. I've always been a numbers person and my passion to make money pushed me into the real estate business. It's been 20 years that I'm into this. However, the 2008 economic recession hit us all badly. I was feeling devastated and wanted to come up with other means of earning instantly. My hard work and research introduced me to the world of internet marketing.

OMG! I know, I know internet marketing is very famous now, but it was a life savior back then. I was in awe to know about the secrets of making money on the internet and really enjoyed sharing it with my friends and family. I strongly believe in growing together. Ever since then, there has been no looking back.

So many of the people know how life changing and mind blowing network marketing can be, and I want you to realize that it might be the only missing piece in your puzzle. Fit that in and you will be living the life you want. Thinking it's too good to be true? Well, it really is. Understanding and integrating the right processes will help you get where you have always wanted to be in life.

Back to my journey;

While I had discovered network marketing, the next step was to choose the niche. Life happened and my husband was discovered with cancer. Ah, those days were so gloomy! It was then I realized the importance of a healthy lifestyle and I decided to make use of the opportunity life had presented me with. I chose the health and fitness niche and I was speechless, I've never been so proud of myself!

I chose my life motto: Look Better, Feel Better, Live Better. Nothing else motivated me. I made a commitment with myself that I'll help people live their dreams along with taking care of what matters the most: their health.

I was determined to work with as many people as possible so they could discover the essentials of life, gain independence and financial freedom. And trust me; I'm blessed with the ability to do it. That's how I became a part of Melaleuca. Melaleuca is a health and wellness company selling home and personal care products."

There's a simple formula for living a better life: if you spend time on things that are fulfilling, the more satisfied life you live.

It doesn't matter if you are a stay at home mum, a business professional or anyone between 30-60 years of age. You are at the right place. If you want support knowing how you can live a healthy life and earn from it while taking care of yourself and your family!

You never know, life can take a U-turn and expose you to a whole new world.

We are eager to expand your universe that's full of possibilities. It gives us so much joy! Know that none of what we have said is an exaggeration to say the least. When we say that there is another realm full of possibilities that will help you creates a successful business, we are true to our heart. It will reveal a world full of treasures that you never knew about. Your mind will blow away, I promise. Open your heart and lift your spirit!

If you are striving to be the best version of you and struggling to achieve your goals, you are headed in the right direction. Your well-being and quality of life should be your first priority. It's time to look beyond the daily grinding process and think what you'd like to become. Envision a better version of yourself and discover your untapped potential. Nothing will ever be more fulfilling. Whatever stage you're in your journey, this book is here to help you. It's always good to ask for some help.

One last thing;

Who doesn't want to be their own boss and live a blissful life on their own terms? Well, I did and I created the vision I believed. I've always wanted to run my own business while being able to raise my family. However, this needed a mix of intelligence, creativity and sheer determination which I didn't know before I had.

Before I became all that I'm today, I kept wondering what life has been trying to teach me. I didn't come up with many possibilities and it wasn't until one fine day when it just clicked. I was jammed by the revelation that I really owed it to myself to step up the game. What had I been waiting for all my life then? A savior or a knight in shining armor to come and save me? Well, all that I was myself! I had been looking in the wrong place all my life. I didn't need to look out, I needed to look within. And that was when I finally found out what needed to be done.

Being a woman myself, I want women to live the life they deserve. While they take care of everyone around them, they need to be caressed for their efforts. Working 9 to 5 will not get you the life you want. Not only are they deprived of their family time, but also stand nowhere when it comes to making ends meet. Becoming a boss or an entrepreneur will help you create a better life for your loved ones.

If you are a mom, I want you to get going immediately. If you are a woman who is looking for ways to make money, I want you to get to work. If you are a woman with some sort of autoimmune disorder and cannot work outside the house, I want you to start something. If you are someone who is already in business but not making enough money, I want you to step up the game. Basically, I want you all to earn enough money even when you are sleeping.

I can't explain how amazing does it feel to have my life all in place. I want you to feel the same way too. Remember, I am here because I want to be, not because I need to be.

Ten years from now, I want you to be able to say you chose this life, and not settle for it. Are you ready to make it happen? You need to establish self-worth that speaks for itself.

References

Ali, S. A. (2016). Top Habits of Highly Connected People: Ways to Engage At-Risk Youth NOW!.

Andersen, S. C., & Nielsen, H. S. (2016). Reading intervention with a growth mindset approach improves children's skills. *Proceedings of the National Academy of Sciences*, *113*(43), 12111-12113.

Burnette, J. L., Pollack, J. M., Forsyth, R. B., Hoyt, C. L., Babij, A. D., Thomas, F. N., & Coy, A. E. (2019). A Growth Mindset Intervention: Enhancing Students' Entrepreneurial Self-Efficacy and Career

Development. *Entrepreneurship Theory and Practice*, 1042258719864293.

Burton, V. (2012). *Successful women think differently: 9 habits to make you happier, healthier, and more resilient*. Harvest House Publishers.

Chase, M. A. (2010). Should coaches believe in innate ability? The importance of leadership mindset. *Quest, 62*(3), 296-307.

Dougherty, D. (2013). The maker mindset. In *Design, make, play* (pp. 25-29). Routledge.

Fisher, M., & Allen, M. (2010). *How to think like a millionaire*. New World Library.

Hymer, B., & Gershon, M. (2014). *Growth mindset pocketbook*. Management Pocketbooks.

Kern, F. (2019). *The Secrets to a Millionaire Mind*. Scribl.

Khalfani, L. (2007). *The Money Coach's Guide to Your First Million: 7 Smart Habits to Building the Wealth of Your Dreams*. McGraw Hill Professional.

Reinhardt, K. S., & Elwood, S. (2019). Promising practices in online training and support: Microlearning and personal learning environments to promote a growth mindset in learners. In *Handbook of research on virtual training and mentoring of online instructors* (pp. 298-310). IGI Global.

Tracy, B. (2017). *Million Dollar Habits: Proven Power Practices to Double and Triple Your Income*. Entrepreneur Press.

www.ingramcontent.com/pod-product-compliance
Lightning Source LLC
Chambersburg PA
CBHW080221220526
45466CB00016B/3319